Santeria and Orishas

An Essential Guide to Lucumi Spells, Rituals and African Orisha Deities along with Their Presence in Yoruba, Voodoo, Hoodoo and Santeria

Your Free Gift (only available for a limited time)

Thanks for getting this book! If you want to learn more about various spirituality topics, then join Mari Silva's community and get a free guided meditation MP3 for awakening your third eye. This guided meditation mp3 is designed to open and strengthen ones third eye so you can experience a higher state of consciousness. Simply visit the link below the image to get started.

https://spiritualityspot.com/meditation

Contents

Part 1: Santería

The Ultimate Guide to Lucumí Spells, Rituals, Orishas, and Practices, Along with the History of How Yoruba Lived On in America

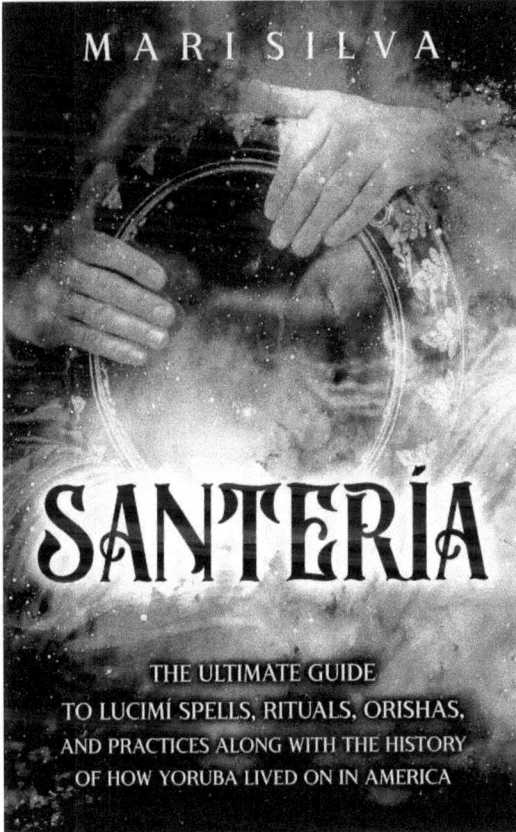

Introduction

Santería is a syncretic religion of African roots, particularly among the Yoruba people of West Africa. In Spanish, Santería means: "The Way of the Saints," but many people refer to it by other names. Some call it La Regla de Ocha, which means "The Order of the Orishas," and others call it La Religíon Lucumí, meaning "The Order of Lucumí."

Santería is not an archaic religion. The religious tradition was developed in Cuba and spread from there to Latin America and the United States. With over five hundred years of history, it is more a lifestyle than a religion. There are millions of practitioners across the Caribbean, United States, South America, and Central America. These adherents are of different backgrounds, and they come from varying walks of life.

Recently, there has been a surge in its popularity, causing more people to want to learn about Santería. This religion's basis is to help you develop personal relationships with the orishas through varying spiritual practices from mediumship to divination and sacrifice. By establishing a relationship with the orisha deities, you place yourself under their protection and wisdom. They can serve as your guide toward personal and professional success. Access to the orishas has many benefits, as you will find in this book.

Naturally, the increasing popularity of Santería has caused many books and guides on the topic to appear on the market. Although many of these resources claim to offer the secrets to the orishas' ways, only a few of them fulfill their promises.

This book is your one-stop-shop for everything there is to know about the orishas and how they can help you live a fulfilled life. Written in simple and straightforward language, it covers the practice of Santería from the very beginning to the present day.

This book explains the origin of the tradition itself and explains how it has become a widespread practice worldwide. From the first to last chapter, you will learn about La Regla de Ocha's fundamentals and the necessary steps toward becoming a devout practitioner.

If you want the power to control your life and connect with your ancestors through the deepest part of your being, Santería is for you. But if you consider this as just another trend to hop on, back out now. It is not a fad. It is a means for you to achieve a direct emotional involvement with life and its many mysteries.

Santería is a religion of mystery, trance, possession, initiation, sacrifice, blood, and sex. This book will take you through it all: page by page. If you would like to learn more, settle down and prepare to experience the orishas in the most intimate ways. Language or race is not a barrier because the deities know their own people.

Let's get to it!

Chapter One: How Yoruba Lived On in America

Santería has African roots in the Yoruba culture, native to Nigeria. The religion was brought to the West by the thousands of African men, women, and children forcibly transported to serve as slaves in the New World. So, it is only fitting that we begin this book by learning more about Yoruba.

The history of Yoruba begins in a place called Ile-Ife. Many regard it as the ancestral kingdom founded by Oduduwa and Obatalá, the two orishas who created the world. Oduduwa is the father of Yoruba. He was a divine king. Obatalá was a god, and he made the first human from clay.

Although most of the Yoruba people live in the South-Western part of Nigeria, smaller groups can be found across different West African countries. Several live in Northern Togo and Benin. The common language of the Yoruba people is also called Yoruba. So, Yoruba is a culture, language, ethnic group, and religion in one.

Yoruba first became internationally known for their trading with the Portuguese. In the early 1800s, they were invaded by the Fulani, pushing them to migrate to the south of Nigeria. During the early 1800s, they formed a peace treaty with the Fulani people.

Eventually, the Yoruba people endured colonization by Britain, but their travels had begun well before then.

Before the arrival of the colonizers, the people lived in urban centers with robust structures in place. A powerful Yoruba kingdom existed in the 8th century. But with the start of the Atlantic slave trade, people from Nigeria and Benin were transported to America and sold as slaves.

Many Africans were shipped across the ocean to different areas across the Americas during the transatlantic slave trade. Many Yoruba people were transported across the entire area, with many landing in regions as diverse as Guyana, Brazil, Venezuela, Surinam, and other places. These places now form what you know as South America.

Enslaved Yorubans arrived in colonies such as Georgia, Florida, South and North Carolina, and other places that now make up the United States. Others ended up in regions such as Hispaniola, Guatemala, Nicaragua, and the West Indies, across the hemisphere that constitutes Central America and the Caribbean.

Up to the 17th century, the Yoruba people were barely partakers in the trans-Atlantic trade. But when a vast conflict started in the Oyo Empire around 1750, they were rendered vulnerable. Consequentially, more and more enslaved people of this tribe arrived in the Americas.

There was a peak between 1826 and 1850 before the slave trade started declining around 1867. According to a historian named S. A. Akintoye, the estimated number of Yorubans that were enslaved and transported across the Atlantic Ocean is approximately 1.2 million. This number represents up to nine percent of the number of Africans forcibly shipped to the Americas.

Although the Yorubans scattered across the new land with other tribes and races, history states that they primarily concentrated in Cuba, Brazil, and Hispaniola, particularly in the Bahia and Saint-Dominique provinces.

Of the 700 000 Africans enslaved and shipped to Saint-Dominique, known today as Haiti, more than 173 000 got captured around the coasts of Benin, Togo, and South-Western Nigeria. And of these 173 000, about 53 000 were Yoruban.

Yoruba people constituted about twelve percent of imported slaves in Bahai. Over eighty percent of them suffered capture during the 19th century. In total, slave traders enslaved and imported 439 000 people of the Yoruba tribe to Brazil's Bahia region. The total number of enslaved Africans was 3.5 million, meaning that Yorubans constituted forty percent of all slaves brought to the Americas.

Since Cuba, Bahia, and Hispaniola had the highest numbers of enslaved Yorubans, it was in these regions that the people stood the risk of losing their culture and religion. They were indeed troubled and almost eradicated, but the people found a way to adapt, thrive, evolve, and survive while leaving a lasting impact on the New World.

The Yoruba people faced a lot of hardships, with more strange faces than familiar ones. They had been forcibly ejected from their homeland to reside in a new country across the ocean. They no longer felt like human beings. The slave masters used them as beasts of burden.

Once they got to the new land, the enslaved people had to modify their religion to adapt for survival. Yoruba underwent a considerable transformation, which led to the formation of Santería. The changes began when they had their first experience with Catholicism in Cuba.

The religion of the enslaved Yorubans expanded across the borders of Cuba, Haiti, Guyana, Brazil, Saint Lucia, Trinidad, and Jamaica, to name a few.

Long before the trans-Atlantic slave trade, the Yoruba nation has always been synonymous with cultural diversity. The Yoruba-dominated regions were (and still are) home to different inter-related cultural groups and independent states with linguistic affiliation. Although each group's dialects were distinct in their own way, they all spoke a standard language.

The standard language, also referred to as Yoruba, is understood by all the various cultural sub-groups. In Nigeria, their groups include Oyo, Egba, Ekiti, Ijebu, Ilaje, Ijesha, Ife, Owo, Ibarapa, Igbomina, Awori, Ondo, Egun, Akoko, Egbado, and Yagba. In other African regions like Benin and Togo, the major sub-groups are Ketu, Ife, Ajase, Sabe, Idaisa, Isa, and Anago. There were also Yorubas in Sierra Leone, Gambia, and other West African countries.

The Yoruba culture's ancestral homeland is in Oyo, Ondo, Ogun, Eko, and a large part of Kwara in Nigeria, plus the formerly known Dahomey region, now the South-Eastern part of Benin.

One thing that is common with all these lands is that they have influenced the different elements of Yoruba mythology and culture, which shaped Santería.

According to one story of creation in the Yoruba culture, the Earth was a bare and lifeless entity before Olorun (God) or Olodumare sent certain heavenly beings to fill it with life. The deity Olorun gave them pieces of dirt, chicken, and a single palm nut to create land, plants, and animals on Earth.

These heavenly beings descended to Earth with a chain and mixed dirt with water to create a solid piece of land. Afterward, they released the chicken and allowed it to scratch the surface to spread the dry land across the entire Earth, creating the world continents.

The single palm nut was sown in the earth, causing plants and other agricultural life to form. In Yoruba mythology, the creation of life on Earth reportedly occurred in Ife, meaning "the source of the spreading." Yoruba believes that Ife was the first home of the orishas and the origin of all human races.

In another version of the creation story, Obatalá, who you will come to know more about in subsequent chapters, was the orisha sent to create the world. Eleduá replaced him with Oduduwa due to disorderly behavior. Apart from these, there are other accounts of the origin story.

There may be several creation accounts, but they all underline Yoruba's versatility and plurality as a culture and religion. It showcases a sort of spiritual resilience put to the test due to the dislocation and enforced re-distribution of Yoruba slaves in the New World. Indeed, it is this resilient spirit that shaped the Yoruba diaspora in America.

As mentioned earlier, the Yorubas are just one of the many ethnicities taken from West Africa for the cross-Atlantic slave trade. Yet, they are one of the few who successfully preserved the fundamental elements of their traditional beliefs. Keep in mind that Santería is not the only Afro-American religion to have Yoruban roots.

The syncretism was achievable solely because of the people's tenacity and the culture's ability to duplicate itself outside of its origin. Several factors contributed to its sustenance across the Atlantic.

The first factor is that the Yorubas believe in a common progenitor. Although the religion is polytheistic and consists of various myths, Yoruba people believe they were the first human race to exist. The people also believe Oduduwa to be the progenitor of the race, this is the foundation of Yoruba.

Regardless of country or dialect, all subgroups that comprise the Yoruba nation firmly believe that they all come from Oduduwa. They carry this belief with them everywhere they go, and it followed them across the ocean into the Americas.

This shows that the origin story is the most fundamental aspect of the culture and religion. It explains how the cultural changes at the Yoruba diaspora's heart formed different modern, syncretic religions.

Another factor that ensured the survival of Yoruba through resilience was the prevalent kinship network among the people. The Roman Catholic Church's strong institution played a substantial role in continuing the Yoruba people's kinship structure, especially in the New World.

Certain Catholic religious doctrines, such as baptism, were excellent mediums for preserving fictive kinship practice among the Yoruba. For example, the participation of enslaved Yorubans in the Catholic ritual of choosing godparents allowed godchildren and godparents to develop an intimate relationship that strengthened the preservation of the family and kinship networks.

They utilized this as an opportunity to show care and support for each other, even though most of them were biologically unrelated. So, Yoruba kinship traditions withstood the adaptation that happened under the colonial and Catholic traditions.

One other Yoruba tradition that was quickly adaptable thanks to the Catholic Church is labor division based on gender. There was a pre-existing gender-based labor division among the Yorubans, and slave owners took advantage of this tradition. The utilization was prevalent on plantations in Bahai and other parts of Brazil.

Males who were enslaved were assigned the most physically tasking labor, such as chopping wood. In contrast, enslaved females performed less-demanding tasks, like constructing fences and harvesting crops.

Before the slave trade, the Yoruba lived in large, populated towns, unlike most of the other ethnic groups that had smaller villages. The initial urban orientation likely played a part in how easily they adapted to life on the plantations, and probably even after the slave trade was abolished. Yoruba settlements such as Oyo, Ife, Ijesha, and others were solid urban structures.

In the Americas, the slave economies used plantation structures with systemic physical layout and organizational workings, similar to the towns and settlements in the urban Yoruba homeland.

Another factor that hugely tipped the odds of sustenance in favor of the Yoruba culture is the people's overabundance in areas most affected by the slave trade and the different intercultural processes established in their homelands.

The common belief is that the traditions, myths, origin, and ideas of the Yoruba culture had already interpenetrated into the Edo and Aja people's cultures. As the Oyo Empire extended its powers, the Yoruba language and culture carried across the towns and villages. Yoruba soon became a common trade language. It also served other commercial purposes in neighboring regions.

An excellent example of the Oyo Empire's expansion of cultural influence is evident in the Dahomey Kingdom—a region that embodied Yoruba and Aja elements. Many Africans from Dahomey were shipped to Bahia from 1770 to 1851, known as the Bight of Benin cycle.

Thanks to the existing diffusion of the Yoruba culture in Bahia, it quickly became dominant among the numerous Black settlements throughout South America and the Caribbean. So, it is safe to say that the voluminous number of enslaved people of Yoruba-descent in several of these areas allowed for the lasting survival of the culture and traditions.

In places like Bahia, where Yorubans made up forty percent of the entire enslaved population, it comes as no surprise that Yoruba-influenced traditions and cultural practices consequently developed in America.

Yoruba has a countless number of deities. The phrase "four hundred and one" is used to provide a concise, understandable figure to the gods' limitless numbers. The damage slavery inflicted on family units led to the fading away of the homeland's most important deities, which gave rise to new, essential gods among those who were enslaved.

Naturally, they couldn't just forgo their deities to worship the white man's god, a god never seen or heard. Yet, they couldn't publicly worship their own gods. How could people call upon their orishas in private while pretending to believe in the unseen God?

Since the enslaved population had to live under the Christian beliefs of their enslavers, they had to worship their orishas under a Catholic pretext. Out of necessity, they syncretized their African pantheistic worship with Catholic beliefs, leading to the birth of several diasporic religions, including Santería.

It is crucial to understand the influences of Yoruba in specific historical events. You will find many of these as focal points as you read on. The Yoruba played a vital role in the abolition of slavery and were even connected to the Black Panther's freedom group.

Culturally, the Yoruba has had a significant influence on the American way of life. This influence reflects in some of the modern expressions of the culture. For example, in her Lemonade music video, Beyoncé was depicted as Osun, the goddess of fertility and beauty. She has made several references to Osun and Yemaya in her songs. She is even said to have dedicated her twins to both deities.

That and other expressions of the Yoruba culture in the modern age highlight its acceptance as a mysterious, virtuous, and influential culture, which is also highly misunderstood.

Today, there may be substantial differences between the Lucumí language used in Santería and the Yoruba language used in modern West Africa. But the truth is that the marriage between Christianity and Yoruba helped the ancestral traditions survive in a foreign land.

Since many of the people enslaved in Cuba were not literate, the native Yoruba language eventually adapted to Creole variations. Cuban-Spanish influenced the pronunciation of several of the Yoruba words and sounds.

In the old notebooks kept by santeros in Cuba, word spellings greatly vary from text to text. The language of Santería no longer adopts the grammar and spelling rules of modern Yoruba. The exchange of ideas and adaptation to the new land has, over time, made the Lucumí people different from their ancestors in Nigeria and other parts of Africa.

A few of the common expressions in Lucumí showcase the influence of Catholicism and Spanish. For instance, the term "kariocha" in Lucumí is the ceremony where a new member is fully initiated into the religion. But in Cuba, you might hear people refer to it as "hacer Santo."

The names of Catholic saints are even used interchangeably with the orishas. Chango is called Santa Barbara and Babalu Aye or Eleguá is called Lazaro. Although calling the deities names of saints isn't as popular as it used to be fifty years ago, many devout followers still use the disguise of saints for their orishas.

Due to this, Santería bears few similarities with the African traditional religion. In Cuba, the enslaved Yorubans had to come together in cabildos (or societies), barracones (slave dorms), cofradias (brotherhood), and solares (shared spaces) to form a bond through iles (house-temples) and ramas (lineages) to practice their religion which the world now knows as La Regla de Ocha.

The next chapter explores Santería in detail and gives an in-depth overview of its origins, beliefs, and hierarchy.

Chapter Two: What is Santería?

Santería comes from Spanish and roughly translates to "The Way of the Saints" or "Devotion to the Saints." Most practitioners of the religion consider "Santería" offensive. Due to specific reasons, they prefer names like Regla de Ocha or La Religion de Lucumí.

So far, you have learned that Santería was born out of necessity. The Spanish tried to impose Christianity on the enslaved people. They fought back by superimposing their orishas on the Catholic saints worshiped in the Church.

The orishas or deities are also called saints or "Santos." Santería combines terminologies and concepts from the Yoruba West African religion and Catholicism, leading to both religions' syncretism.

These are a few of the things explained and discussed in the previous chapter. Still, this chapter will delve into them a little deeper so that you can understand this religion and its sanctity.

The Yoruba people brought to Cuba did not lose their pre-existing traditional religious beliefs. Instead, they remained firm in their beliefs because those were the only things that reminded them of their homeland.

Around the early 18th century, the Catholic Church allowed them to create societies known as cabildos. These were modeled after the existing religious guilds in Spain. The cabildos were exclusively for the Yoruba people and other African ethnicities. They were meant to be a source of entertainment and for the reconstruction of their African heritage. Through these, different aspects of their traditional beliefs and practices were modified.

Enslaved Yorubans, in particular, could practice ancient religious ceremonies in the cabildos, along with other secular and religious traditions from different parts of West Africa. It led to the amalgamation of their pantheon of orishas (gods) with their Christian masters' pantheon of Catholic saints.

To worship their gods without the masters finding out, enslaved Yorubans appointed a Saint's Day for each of the orishas. Thus, when slave owners saw the Yorubans participating in the celebration of a Saint's Day, they had no idea the orishas were being worshipped instead.

Because the slave owners did not allow the practice of African traditional religions, the enslaved population found a way around that by disguising their orishas as Catholic saints, while passing their traditions and identities down from one generation to another in secret.

As a result, orishas and saints are now used interchangeably by members of the Regla de Ocha community. The connection between the Christian saints and Lucumí orishas remains a core part of Cuba's religious culture.

When enslaved Yorubans arrived in Cuba, they addressed each other as "Oluku mi," which loosely translates to "My friend" in the English language. Later, it became ascribed to the religion they practiced in secret. Soon, it would become "Lucumí," the name that the practitioners of Regla de Ocha call one another.

Initially, the word "Santería" was the Spanish word used to deride the followers over their devotion to the patron saints and their seeming neglect of God. Therefore, many members of the community consider it offensive enough to avoid its use.

Many reject the term Santería because they believe people overemphasize the Catholic and syncretic elements of the religion. Over the past years, many Afro-Caribbean religious community members would instead call it La Regla de Lucumí or La Regla de Ocha.

There are common misconceptions about Santería that affect outsiders' perception of the devotees. Correcting the misperception is key to understanding this religion in depth.

One misconception is that Afro-Cubans combined two religions to form one. A more accurate way to think about syncretism is that both beliefs are parallel to each other. The practitioners of Santería do not see any contradiction between Catholicism and the Yoruba religion. Instead, they believe that they are complementary to each other. One does not invalidate the other.

If you practice Lucumí, you may refer to yourself as Catholic, attend mass, and have the right to baptize your children. At the same time, you keep worshipping the orishas in your ilé, the Yoruba word for "home." You may also choose to worship in the home of a religious elder. That choice is entirely up to you.

The key is to understand that the Catholic saints and the orishas are not identical, but there are similarities.

Another misconception is Lucumí is a polytheistic religion. Again, this is inaccurate. The devotees believe in one Supreme Being as the God of all that exists. Just as Christians believe in the holy trinity, the Yorubas believe that the Supreme Being manifests in three different ways, which makes them refer to God as Olorun, Olodumare, and Olofi.

They believe that these three names are the three representations of God. Olorun means the owner of heaven. The name is a manifestation of God, who appears to the world as the Sun. Olodumare means the Father and the Creator of all that exists in the universe. Through the warmth bestowed on the Sun, you can bask in the glorious world that Olodumare created for all human beings. Olofi, as the third manifestation of the supreme, is the version the orishas directly communicate with to make your wishes and requests known.

Olofi teaches the gods everything they need to live respectful, righteous, moral, and fulfilling lives on Earth. The orishas are intermediaries between Earth and the heavens. They are not the ones you worship. Instead, they are the channel through which you communicate your needs to Olorun. They watch and guide your actions and also report them to Olofi.

Olofi also grants the orishas spiritual energy to maintain balance, harmony, and spiritual righteousness in the world.

The orishas once existed on Earth as humans, and after death, they achieved semi-divine status. If you are already familiar with Catholicism, you will realize that this is similar to the Catholic saints' stories. It is another reason why the Yoruba religion meshed smoothly with Catholicism.

Regardless of syncretism, followers of the orishas never confuse them for the saints and vice versa. As a santero or santera, you must understand that the orishas are complex and mystical beings. You cannot express their essence in a single form or image. Know that they exist in your life in the form of divine energy that lives within and around you.

Outsiders often call Regla de Ocha a primitive religion. Some argue that it is esoteric. The reality is that it is neither of these things. The Yoruba who founded the Lucumí religion were a highly civilized people with an illustrious culture. Before they arrived in the New World, they had a powerful and wealthy kingdom.

The enslaved Yorubans possessed a profound sense of morals and ethics, which are reflected in the practices of Lucumí. They were excellent philosophers. You won't find a unified body of text that serves as the sacred book of Lucumí because the religion was passed down through oral tradition by trusted priests and priestesses.

Nonetheless, there are sacred stories called "patakis" through which you can embody the teachings of the orishas. One of the requirements of religious training in the Lucumí community is that new members study and memorize the patakis.

To a certain extent, aspects of Santería are kept secret to protect their sanctity from outsiders, but that does not make the religion primitive or esoteric.

If you choose to become an initiate of the religion, you will find the principles relatively easy to grasp. In many ways, the point of mastering the orishas' ways is so that you can live in harmony with yourself, the world around you, and the spirits of your ancestors.

Nonmembers usually depict Santería as a bloodthirsty and evil religion that involves the worship of demons through blood rituals. Some people even think that the practitioners seek to do evil to others. It may be easy to say that this is just another misconception, but it is much more than that.

It is a racist and colonial depiction by outsiders who don't understand the complexities of African traditional religions. Santeros and santeras have a strong sense of cooperation. They work together to help others and lift people out of poverty and poor health.

Santería's blood sacrifices and rituals are necessary for blessings, prosperity, good health, and longevity. Animal sacrifice is a prerequisite for initiation into the religion. And this is because initiation represents a birth into a new life. When you choose to become an initiate of Regla de Ocha, you choose a new destiny and path.

Birth is associated with blood. For your patron orisha to choose and accept you, they have to consume the blood of a sacrificed animal. Without blood sacrifice, you cannot truly become an initiate of Santería.

If there are no animal sacrifices, there is no religion because the blood sacrifices are part of what make up the foundation of Lucumí. The good thing is that the Supreme Court of the United States has upheld Santería practitioners' right to perform animal sacrifices.

Now, let's get to what you must know about the beliefs in Santería.

The first is that there is just one God. As mentioned earlier, Santería is not the polytheistic religion many think it is. Its followers believe in one God, the creator of the universe called Olodumare.

Confusion often arises because the followers refer to orishas as gods. In reality, the orishas are not gods. They are aspects of God that manifest in the earthly world to fulfill his wishes and commands for human beings.

Every individual is a child of an orisha. While there are tons of them, some are more known than others. Ogun, Eleguá, Yemaya, and Oshún are a few of Santería's most popular deities. All the orishas are of equal importance to followers, despite the level of popularity.

African traditional religions generally emphasize ancestor worship. Santería initiates and practitioners do this as well. Reverence to ancestors is a fundamental part of the religion. So, initiates carry out prayers and libation to their ancestors before every ceremony. During ceremonies, you should know and mention the names of every member of your family who has passed to the realm of the ancestors and the names of your religious ancestors.

Santería followers have adopted European practices such as Mesa Blanca and espiritismo. Within the context of these practices, there is no hierarchy. Every person is expected and encouraged to develop mediumship abilities to channel the orishas and ancestors. Songs are sung, and prayers are chanted to invite those from the spiritual realm to communicate with those on Earth.

Santería is a community with a clearly defined hierarchy. It is not something you can do on your own. Trying to practice Santería on your own with no guidance from an enlightened priest or priestess will only lead to failure.

Trained santeros and santeras are the only ones who can lead and perform ceremonies. They belong to an ancient community of priests with a historical lineage in the community. Usually, they practice and train together for different roles in an ilé (a religious house). You may also refer to them as Babalawos, the Yoruba word for priest.

Initiation does not automatically qualify you as a priest. To become a babarisha or Babalawo, you must train and study for years. Naturally, there can be good and bad priests. After all, humans are inherently good and evil.

Akpwon is the title of the community religious singer with knowledge of all the spiritual songs. Omo Ana plays the sacred drums that come with Tambors. Aborishas are non-initiated members of Santería living together in a religious house.

Several specialize in making religious foods, and others are herb specialists. Other roles in the community include throne makers, beaders, and several others. A newly initiated priest is called Iyawo.

Finally, the oriate/oba are the most skilled Babalawos of the community. They are well-versed in divination. They know the diloggún in and out, which makes them the mouthpieces of the orishas. They lead the most important ceremonies.

Divination is fundamental to Santería. At some point in your new journey as a follower of this religion, you will find yourself at Ifá's feet. The diloggún is the tool of Ifá through which followers get guidance from the god. You may also use it to communicate to the orisha assigned to you by Olodumare. In a later chapter, you will learn more about how to divine and communicate with the orishas.

Two vital concepts are central to the practice of Santería. They are at the very center of its core beliefs. The first is Ashé (also called Ase, Axe, Ache). Simply put, Ashé is your life force. It is the spiritual energy bestowed upon you by Olodumare. Without it, you cannot exist. Whether you are a Santería practitioner or not, you have Ashé. It gives you the wisdom to see things that the ordinary eyes cannot see and the power to create. There would be no existence without it.

The second concept is iwa pele, meaning gentle character. Every Santería follower understands the importance of iwa pele. Initiated or not, you must grasp its meaning. Living with good nature and grace is the key to finding your purpose in life.

As a spiritual being, you are responsible for making the best of the life with which Olodumare has blessed you. It would help if you strived to evolve and improve at every point of your mortal life. You are encouraged to find your faults, analyze them, and work on becoming better.

Striving to be a good person with a gentle character is a must if you want to practice Santería. It would help if you were deliberate in your efforts and actions toward other people. It is what iwa pele entails. By striving, you can change the flow of Ashé around you.

If you cannot understand and adopt the concept of iwa pele dictating the energy flow around you, being a santero or santera means nothing. Titles are inconsequential unless you learn to cultivate Ashé and iwa pele. In chapter four, you will find out more about acquiring both.

Animal sacrifice is often emphasized by those who know little about Santería, when in reality, it is just a tiny part of your routine. Offerings to orishas are not only made with the blood of animals. You may appease them with flowers, fruit, candles, water, or prepared food items.

Unless it is for initiation, it is pretty rare for animals to be used for sacrifice. Nonetheless, it is an essential part of the tradition. While some may postulate that animal sacrifice is cruelty, it is not intended as such.

Followers don't just slaughter animals and throw them away. More often than not, sacrificed animals are consumed. The animals are also slaughtered in the same way that Muslims and Jews kill them for halal meat. Prayers accompany sacrifices, and people who attend the ceremonies eat the slaughtered animal.

The practitioners of Santería have no temples or churches where they meet together to worship the orishas. Generally, the house of a santero is their temple. Everyone does not worship the same orishas. So, each santero sets up a temple in their home for the orisha they follow.

There is no sacred book or list of commandments for everyone to follow. But as a santera, you may seek guidance and advice from your assigned orisha. Each orisha has its dos and don'ts, and its followers must master these.

Songs accompany ceremonies in Santería. As a budding practitioner, you must learn the songs to participate in any ceremony and cultivate a powerful Ashé. There are different ceremonies. Some are simple, while others are complicated and critical.

Tambor de Fundamento or Ana is a very public ritual drumming ceremony. Anyone can attend and participate in the ceremony. Still, the uninitiated are not allowed to stay in the front, approach the drums, or lead the ceremony, but they can sing the songs along with the initiates. Everyone at the ceremony must sing to build up Ashé.

The drums used in this ceremony are consecrated, and an orisha called Ana lives within them. The drums speak because of the orisha Ana. The point of the Tambor is to invoke the orishas and bring them down to Earth.

Initiated priests serve as vessels through which the gods communicate to everyone for a short time. They impart knowledge and give positive advice to all those that partake in Ana.

Now, one thing about Santería is that you can practice the religion with or without being initiated. Initiation is not compulsory for those who don't want it, but if you're going to be an initiate, know that initiation takes between a week and a year.

The initial period is seven days, and during this period, different rituals and ceremonies are executed. This period is then followed by one year of a code of conduct that requires strict adherence. Often, it includes wearing white and sacred beads and bangles.

During this time, you are not to have physical contact with the uninitiated. You cannot drink alcohol, use makeup, shave, or eat together with everyone at the table. You cannot go out after dark, hug non-initiates, walk barefooted, visit crowded places, take anything from anyone, or shake hands with people.

You may not take pictures or have your photo taken or attend any form of parties. All your meals and drinks must be from a unique bowl and cup that must be with you at all times.

The purpose of this is to keep you completely pure during the period that you study and try to understand the orishas. You must also cover your head at all times. Essentially, that first year signifies your rebirth period and is the start of your new journey and life.

After the year-long initiation is over, you become a santero or santera, depending on your gender. You must continue to follow specific taboos and restrictions for the rest of your life. Taboos are specific to individuals because they relate to you as a person. As noted before, new initiates are called Iyawo, which translates to "new bride" in Yoruba. Technically, you become a bride of the gods when you go through initiation.

Becoming an initiate means making a life-long commitment to a particular god, and this deity becomes central to your life and consciousness. From the moment of initiation, you become committed to offering intermittent sacrifices to the orisha ruling your head. As a newly-ordained priest, you now have the power to initiate your own godchildren.

Sometimes, male priests are initiated to conduct divination through the oracle, not undergo possession. These priests later become the most-revered Babalawos of the community.

Usually, devotees set up an altar in their home for orisha worship. The deities are represented by stones and other sacred emblems, placed inside jars, lidded calabash or gourds, tureens, or bowls. These are embodiments of Ashé, the divine power.

Each of the hundreds of orishas has myths, foods, colors, numbers, dances, songs, and dance rhythms that you must learn as a devotee. Suppose you attend a sacred dance ceremony for santeros. In that case, you can quickly identify an orisha's manifestation by the movements of the medium.

There is an annual anniversary of initiation. This yearly tradition involves a sacrifice to the orisha that rules your head. Also, there are annual festivals held to honor each of the seven most-revered orishas; these are called the cycle of tambores, and they coincide with the corresponding saint's day in the Roman Catholic religion. Again, this reflects the syncretistic relationship that birthed Lucumí.

The next chapter gives in-depth information on the orishas, but know that Lucumí has seven main orishas that are the most important in the religion. There is a form of hierarchy that guides their worship.

Patakis are myths and legends that tell the stories of the orishas. As a santero or santera, you must understand that these legends may not be literally true. Still, recognize that the essence of patakis is to help you gain knowledge that can dictate your journey in life.

Santería has little to no fixed dogma. Therefore, the recitation and interpretation of the patakis may vary from individual to individual. Regions also play a role in the kind of knowledge you acquire through the myths of the gods.

One particular pataki explains the relationship between Chango (Shango) and Ogun (Oggun). It concerns the anger they shared. Unbeknownst to Chango, Ogun started an affair with their mother, a severe crime in the tradition. Another god, Eleguá, became aware of the incestuous relationship and alerted the gods' leader, Obatalá.

Obatalá ended the relationship and gave an extreme punishment to Ogun. When Chango found out about the affair between his brother and mother, he decided to exact revenge. He did this by seducing Ogun's beautiful wife. This caused a rift that still hasn't been fixed between both brothers. Thus, they are always in combat with each other. Another version of this particular pataki says that another orisha Orunla was birthed due to the union.

There may be variations of the patakis, but that doesn't change the lessons they are supposed to teach Santería devotees. More will be discussed on patakis in another chapter.

Santería, as you know now, was born from the spirit of resistance shown by the enslaved Yorubans, who were forced to adapt to their new environment to prevent the eradication of their traditional beliefs and religion.

Think of Catholicism as the root in which the Yoruba traditions' seeds had to be buried for a beautiful flower to grow. The Lucumí then understood that for trees and plants to survive a violent storm, they have to bend and be flexible. Any tree or plant that does otherwise would be ripped from its roots to die.

Thanks to the flexibility of the enslaved Yorubans, knowledge of the ways of the orishas survived, and people continue to benefit from them.

Next, let's learn more about the orishas themselves!

Chapter Three: The Orisha Gods

The deities worshipped in the Lucumí religion are called orishas, the Yoruba word for gods. As you have learned, the gods are representatives of Olodumare. He created and sent them to the world to supervise and help humankind. He also gave them divine powers so that they could perform their tasks excellently.

Orishas are mediators between the Earth and the heavens. They are your medium of communication with Olodumare himself. Each divine god relates to certain aspects of nature and has control over aspects of human existence.

The orishas may possess virtue and other divine qualities, but they also have human-like traits. Their personalities, characters, and mannerisms are similar to those of human beings. They are a mix of the celestial and the worldly.

Some are described as having calm, tranquil, and serene characters, which reflect in their relationship with humans. Others embody what it means to be human. They are sometimes hotheaded, erratic, and whimsical. At other times, they are gentle, generous, and rational. A good example is Yemaya, who the aborishas say is like the tide—sometimes high, sometimes low. That description may very well apply to all the gods.

The human-like attributes of the orishas are pivotal to the start and growth of Santería. Humans find it easy to relate to the gods because they have virtues and flaws. They are not perfect, even if they have divine powers. They aren't excellence personified, so you don't have to strive to be that way either.

They are on a level that you can relate to and they will help you to understand and accept your virtues and flaws. Therefore, you can conveniently develop a bond with your deity. By identifying with one particular orisha, you can form an interpersonal relationship that will help you for as long as you live.

Remember that the exact number of orishas is unknown. Several figures are based purely on speculation, so they don't stand a chance with orisha worshippers. There is a specific list of orishas that are recognized, worshiped, and followed by everyone, despite region or anything else, in Yorubaland.

Some are known and worshipped in towns and villages. In the New World, the widely-known orishas survived even in the strange land. On the other hand, regional deities became lost due to a lesser presence among the enslaved Yorubans.

Those orishas that survived the cross-Atlantic journey reinstated themselves in the new world and continue to stay relevant. Yet, other changes were made to ensure complete survival. In the Americas, specifically Cuba, orishas had to play roles that fit in with the new society's structure.

Those that no longer served practical purposes were soon forgotten. Some had their ranks diminished, and others were turned into avatars of other orishas with whom they bore similarities. The more powerful ones absorbed the weaker and lesser-known gods in ceremonies known as "oro."

For example, when a priest of the orisha Aganju is to be ordained, the initiation ceremony is labeled as Shango (Chango), but the oro is really for Aganju. priests and priestesses for the orisha Erinle are ordained through the orisha Yemaya.

Some regional orishas survived eradication and were able to retain followers to an extent. Still, knowledge of their existence isn't as widely known. Some orishas withstood slavery over time but have since become lost because they didn't survive the after-effects of change.

An excellent example is the orisha Oshumare, the divine goddess of the rainbow. After the death of her last priestess, who was knowledgeable in her rituals and sacrifices, no one in Cuba remembers her.

Orishas are categorized into two principal categories, which consist of those from time immemorial and those that attained semi-divinity after death. The first category of orishas is celestial, while the second category is terrestrial. The terrestrial orishas were once ordinary people and are historical heroes. In certain instances, the deified ancestors usurped the older deities' worship and stuck to the established traditional system. The case of Jakuta and Shango is a good example.

During slavery, orishas also underwent a transformation process that either affected their pantheon status, altered their personality or character, diminished, increased, or eliminated their dominion, or even gained new elements that had nothing to do with their Yoruba origin.

Oshún was a river goddess in Yorubaland, and she eventually became the sole "owner" of the Cuban river. Yemaya (Yemoja) was worshipped primarily in the Ogun River in Nigeria. In Cuba, she became the "owner" of the seas. Oduduwa was syncretized with Saint Manuel, which led to him becoming the "king of the dead." Erinle was given the primary role attributed to Saint Raphael, and she became a "divine doctor." Yewa was a minor goddess and the lagoon ruler, and she was moved to the cemetery.

The result of the syncretization is that the orishas soon came to be known as Santos. As mentioned earlier, initiation into the Santería community is called hacer santos—making the saint. It is held yearly on the anniversary of the saints with which the orishas are associated.

Orishas are adorned with paraphernalia relating to the catholic saints. The devotees set up tronos (altars) for rituals. These often contain symbols of Yoruba and the catholic saints' sculptures. For example, Shango's altar is typically set up with swords attributed to Saint Barbara.

The deities have individual likes and dislikes. Each has a preference for a specific food, color, beads, and other related adornments. Depending on which orisha rules your head, you must conform to specific codes.

The orishas also receive different animals as sacrifices. Several even have taboos in terms of food and behaviors. If you choose to worship a particular orisha, you are expected never to violate their taboos. Otherwise, you may invoke the wrath of a god.

Also, there is a specific number associated with the worship of each orisha. This number represents the number of items to be given in offering by a follower. Many require you to dress in a particular way, speak moderately, and avoid foul language in their vicinity. Sometimes, an orisha may even forbid sexual intercourse and promiscuousness.

Below is a description of the seven main orishas that takes their characteristics, attributes, and roles into account. The narrative is both from a Yoruba and Santería perspective.

Obatalá (Obbatalá): Owner of All Heads

- Catholic Saint: Our Lady of Mercy
- Manifestation: White Horse
- Day of the week: Sunday/Thursday
- Associated number: 8
- Color: White/Silver
- Feast Day: September 24
- Animals: Goat, Rooster, Hen, Pigeon, and Guinea Fowl
- Taboos: Salt, Liquor, and Palm Oil

Obatalá is the god of creation and peace. Olodumare gave him the job of sculpting humankind. His name loosely translates to "the king of white cloth," but what this means is that he personifies purity.

According to his pataki (myth), Olodumare sent him down at the beginning of time with instructions to create the Earth. He gave him a chicken and dry dirt and told him to create land with it. When Obatalá got to Earth, he poured the soil into a pile in the center of the waters that covered the Earth. Then, he released the chicken on top of it.

Naturally, the chicken started scratching and spreading the dirt until a vast part of water became land, and the Earth took shape. Once the world and continents had formed, Olofi instructed Obatalá to create human beings. He obeyed and used clay to make human bodies and added heads to the bodies after he was done. That is one reason why he is regarded as the owner of all heads. A variation of this pataki was narrated in the first chapter.

In another pataki, Obatalá saved humankind from extinction. One day, the orishas had a party and neglected to invite Yemaya. She was furious, and, in her anger, she awakened the oceans from their very depth and flooded the universe. Out of terror, humans ran to Obatalá to save them. He went to Yemaya and soothed her to make her retreat. She did, out of respect to him. As the creator of the world, Obatalá is the only one allowed to end it.

Orisha Obatalá owns all that is white. He also owns the head and all the thoughts and dreams contained within it. His colors are white and silver, so he owns all silver and white metals. His tree is the ceiba tree. He likes cocoa butter, marble eggs, cotton, snails, and cascarilla.

To pay tribute to Obatalá, you may offer him white rice, meringues, rice pudding, white custard, black-eyed peas, and fruit, like apples, pears, malanga (taro root), sweet potato, and pomegranates. He hates salt, so you can never add that to his foods or offerings.

Obatalá is the son of Olodumare. He was sent down to Earth to govern the planet and do good. He is calm, gentle, wise, and understanding. He embodies peace and harmony and demands obedience and good behavior from his children. You cannot swear or curse in his presence, and nudity is not allowed. Children of Obatalá do not drink alcohol because it is one of his taboos. They must always be dressed in white, with a white eleke (beaded necklace) because that is his color.

His children worship him using a white or silver porcelain sopera kept on the altar in an ile. Obatalá, through his powers, protects his followers and devotees against paralysis, dementia, and blindness. Since he is the owner of all heads, every Lucumí is indirectly ordained to him regardless of the orisha they worship.

Obatalá has many caminos (paths), which means that you can manifest him through different avatars. He can be male or female, depending on his path. Obatalá Ayaguna, Obatalá Obu Moro, and Obatalá Ocha Grinan are all male avatars. On the other hand, Obatalá Alaguema, Obatalá Obanla, and Obatalá Ochanla are female avatars.

Altogether, Obatalá possesses 24 Caminos. A few know him as a father, and others know him as a mother. The children of Obatalá are calm, trustworthy, and peaceful, but they are also strong-willed. They are often reserved and have few complaints about the world.

Because their father is the owner of all heads, they are intelligent and have an affinity for education. Obatalá loves order and cleanliness. The environment you worship him in must be calm and noiseless at all times. Obatalá loves his children and is patient with them, but he also demands obedience and respect. Tall, majestic mountains are the symbols of Obatalá.

Whether you are ordained to him during initiation or not, you can always seek guidance and intervention from him during trying times. Even when other orishas turn a deaf ear, Obatalá will listen and intercede on your behalf because he created human beings.

Eshu-Elegba (Eleguá): Lord of the Crossroads

- Catholic Saint: Holy Child of Atocha, Anima Sola, and Saint Anthony of Padua
- Manifestation: Old Man, Child
- Day of the week: Monday
- Associated number: 3, 7, 11, and 21
- Color: Red, Black, and White
- Feast Day: June 3
- Animals: He-Goats, Chickens, Roosters, Turtles, and Agouties
- Taboos: Palm Kernel Oil, Whistling

Eleguá has different meanings. He is called Eshu, Esu, Papa Legba, and Elegba by different people. However, there is a difference between Eshu and Eleguá which will be explained. He is sometimes depicted as an older man, and at other times, as a child.

He represents the beginning and end of life. He is everywhere. You can find him at crossroads and corners, the rivers, mountains, seashores, curbs, sidewalks, and at the door of your home. Wherever there is a human manifestation, you will find Eleguá there.

He is the bridge between good and evil. He represents opening and closing, which is why he opens and closes religious functions. Many people know him as the trickster because he likes to pull a quick one on people. It is safe to say that he has a childlike nature as he enjoys toys and candies.

Despite all this, he is a prominent and influential orisha. He is a warrior orisha, just like Ogun, Oshún, and Ochosi. Without his permission, you cannot open the gateway to other orishas. Therefore, his name is the first to be mentioned in any religious ceremony.

As noted, he is centered between the forces of good and those of evil. When you behave according to divine law, he uses the forces of good to grant you blessings. On the contrary, if you act unorderly, he opens the pathway for the forces of evil to render punishment.

Eleguá enjoys all things associated with child's play, such as balls, toy soldiers, kites, keys, straw hats, silver coins, and shepherds' crooks. He mostly dresses in red and black, but he sometimes adds a touch of white. He may even add colonial-style knee britches to his clothing sometimes. On his head, he wears a red cap or straw hat. He dances playfully and wants attention from others.

Apart from candy, he enjoys foods like coconut, cigars, aguardiente (alcohol), white cooking wine, smoked fish, smoked hutia meat, and red palm oil. On Mondays, his devotees offer foods he likes to pay tribute to him. Note that he detests palm kernel oil.

To receive Eleguá, you need to divine with a Babalawo or Santera and find out what he wants from you. Sometimes, you may receive Eleguá alone or with other orisha warriors. He is channeled through a special ceremony that involves preparing a stone representing him and charging his Ashé.

The stone is usually shaped like a head with outer layers made from cement with cowrie shell eyes and mouths. Eleguá resides in a shallow clay dish in ile, placed behind the door. When you successfully receive Eleguá, you become a half-initiate or Medio asentados. You cannot perform all the duties of a fully-initiated olorisha. Still, you have established an essential commitment to the religion and the orisha.

Eleguá's eleke typically contains one red bead, then one black bead, in repeated patterns. This necklace design and the colors represent beginning and end, life and death, and war and peace. Eleguá is the lord of the crossroads because he is pivotal to every single decision you make in life. Things go smoothly when you seek his assistance before making any decisions.

But he also has a predisposition to putting obstacles in people's paths. Life takes unexpected and negative turns when he does this. As a Lucumí, you must establish and maintain a good relationship with Eleguá because you cannot achieve anything without him.

Now to the slight difference between Eshu and Eleguá. They are two sides of one coin. They are opposite, but not separate. Think of Eshu as who Eleguá sees when he looks in the mirror. He is more of an alter ego with a wilder and less controllable side. He is unpredictable and mischievous.

Unlike Eleguá, eshu's tricks are malicious and harmful. He would be the Santería equivalent of the devil if such a thing were recognized in this religion. Most practitioners don't keep eshu in the house because of his antics. Still, he is a mighty deity.

Traditionally, no one gets crowned with eshu as the owner of their head, while many people get Eleguá. You don't have to wear elekes assigned to eshu, but Eleguá has concentrated elekes. Unlike Eleguá, Eshu likes to eat, and you can calm him with food.

Sometimes, Santería practitioners place wooden bowls of food scraps outside their homes so that Eshu can eat and be calm. At other times, Eleguá is the one who keeps him under control. Both understand each other almost perfectly and are together at all times.

Metaphorically, you may think of Eshu and Eleguá as opposites. Eshu represents the negative, whereas Eleguá represents the positive. Eshu is the darkness, and Eleguá is the light. Both exist together to create and maintain balance in life because no one appreciates the positive without the negative.

Life is a blend of good and evil, and devotees understand that. It would be outright defamation to say that Eshu is evil. He is just not as refined as the other orishas or Eleguá. Most practitioners consider him a part of Eleguá rather than a deity in his own right.

Regardless of how you view the Eshu/Eleguá dichotomy, the bottom line is that one cannot exist without the other. Just as you can't understand daylight until you've experienced nighttime, you must strive to understand both orishas.

Shango (Chango): Lord of Fire, Lightning, and Thunder

- Catholic Saint: Santa Barbara
- Manifestation: Double-Headed Axe
- Day of the week: Friday
- Associated number: 6
- Color: Red, White
- Feast Day: December 4

- Animals: Rams, Turtles, Roosters, Young Bulls, Quails, and Guinea Hens
- Taboos: None

Shango is the god of fire, lightning, thunder, and war, but he is not just about rage. He is also the god of music, dancing, and drumming. He is the symbol of male virility and beauty, power, and passion. His favorite colors are red and white, and his sacred necklace is made of alternating white and red beads.

Saint Barbara is Shango's syncretized saint because of the similarities between the two. According to catholic lore, she is a fiercely brave and independent woman dressed in a red and white costume, with a sword and a crown. And that is the same way that Shango is depicted in Yoruba lore.

Some people find it surprising that a very powerful male orisha is parallel to a female saint. The fact is that both share similar stories. According to catholic lore, Santa Barbara's torturer was struck down by lightning, and that is Shango's favorite weapon.

There is a pataki about Shango, which deepens the similarities. On one occasion, he had to dress in women's clothes, which he got from the goddess Oya to evade and escape from those who wanted to kill him. The association of Shango with Saint Barbara shows that both male and female devotees can channel their powers. Gender apart, new initiates crowned with Shango get him as their religious father in the spiritual realm.

Shango is one of those historical heroes that were given divine status after death. As a human, he was a king in old Oyo, one of the Yoruba people's ancestral homelands. He exemplifies many qualities associated with human kings. He is brave, fierce, proud, intelligent, and hardworking, a mighty warrior, and above all, a leader.

He likes to lead, so he doesn't have to follow orders from any other orishas. He makes a superb friend, and he is a master of healing and divination. But like all the orishas, he also has imperfections that make him relatable. These flaws remind us of the time he spent on Earth.

Shango is a known womanizer and a libertine, to an extent. He is seductive, manipulative, and charming. Many describe him as a sweet talker, although wasteful and egoistical. He is prone to losing his temper and becoming arrogant and domineering when tested.

He is also a good father to his children, as long as they are obedient. Disobedience makes him critical, and he punishes his children who don't live up to his expectations. Like their father, the children of Shango are intelligent, strong-willed, energetic, fiery, vibrant, and sometimes self-absorbed. They tend to have short tempers, although they also like to party, flirt, dance, and generally have a good time. They have magnetic charisma and have no trouble courting attention.

Shango has exciting relationships with a few of the orishas. He had numerous lovers during his time on Earth. Still, the most notable were his relationships with Oya, Oba, and Oshún at different times.

Remember that Shango and Ogun are brothers? Well, Oya is the wife he seduced away from his brother. When he goes to war, he prefers to be accompanied by Oya because she has an equally fierce nature. When you hear the sound of thunder followed by lightning, that is an indication that Shango and Oya are riding into battle together in the heavens.

Oshún is a more sensual and seductive goddess, and she was Shango's favorite lover. Oba was his least-liked lover. She cut off her ear in an attempt to court Shango's love and attention, but she failed. After that, she retired to the cemetery with a broken heart.

Several legends say that Shango was Yemaya and Agayú's son, but she gave him to Obatalá to raise him on Earth and make him a king. Another variation of the pataki says that Yemaya was his foster mother and Obatalá (female avatar) was his biological mother.

Shango owns the bata drums, and he is the best dancer among the orishas. According to one pataki, this was not always the case. In the past, Orula was the best dancer, and Shango was the best diviner/healer. They then agreed to exchange their talents because of Shango's love of dancing.

The foods he enjoys are okra, cornmeal, red palm oil, and bananas. He dresses in a red shirt with white trimmings and red satin pants. On his head, there is always a crown depicting his royalty. He lives in a shallow lidded bowl called a batea, which you may place on a wooden pedestal.

With his powers, he protects his devotees from burns and death by fire. His symbol is a double-headed axe representing swift justice. Any Shango follower can invoke him by shaking a maraca and praying at his altar.

Ogun: The Lord of Iron and War

- Catholic Saint: Saint Peter
- Manifestation: Solitary Ironmonger or Blacksmith
- Day of the week: Tuesday, Wednesday
- Associated number: 3, 7, 21
- Color: Green, Black, Red, and Brown
- Feast Day: June 29
- Animals: Dogs, He-Goats, Roosters, Pigeons, Agouties, Hunted Animals
- Taboos: None

Ogun is the iron warrior. He owns all metals and minerals, particularly iron. He is associated with metal tools, machetes, knives, firearms, and weapons generally, as well as the mountains. His portrayal is often as a solitary ironmonger or blacksmith living all alone in the forest.

When the orishas were sent down to Earth, Olofi instructed Ogun to clear the forests with his iron tools. The patakis about him say that his father was Obatalá and his mother was Yemú. Eleguá and Ochosi were considered his brothers. A few sacred stories tell us that Shango was his half-brother.

According to a pataki, Ogun loved his mother and sought to know her carnally. Eleguá was, however, on the lookout, and he always stopped him. On one fateful day, he managed to evade Eleguá, and forced himself on his mother. Unfortunately for him, Obatalá caught him in the act.

Before his father could punish him, he cursed himself. He promised Obatalá he would retire to the wilderness and live there for the rest of eternity. He also said he would entirely devote himself to work. In the forests, only Ochosi, his brother, and great hunter saw him occasionally.

Day and night, Ogun worked miserably and unhappily. As a result, he started spreading ofoshe (magic) around the Earth to create tragedy and discord. To save humans from his actions, the goddess Oshún intervened by seducing him with her beauty and sensuality. Once he met Oshún, Ogun became calm and let go of his bitterness. He used to be married to Oya, but Shango snatched her from him. This led to them becoming enemies to the present day.

Ogun is the owner of everyone who works with metal, including mechanics, soldiers, police officers, engineers, surgeons, and many others. He is in tune with the world's secrets and can perform powerful magic when there is a need for it.

He is brash, brusque, and violent, but there is a quiet side to him. He bonds well with plants and animals, and that makes him a great farmer and hunter. He owns all keys and locks, chains, and jails, and everything is built on his foundation.

The orisha also takes charge of labor and construction. Ogun is in charge of the technology needed for human evolution and progress in the world. Traditionally, he is depicted as a man wearing a tight-fitting cap on his head with a bare chest, and a pouch slung across one shoulder. He has a belt with a lining or fringe of palm fibers (mariwo) around his waist, which offers him protection against evil. He, together with Eleguá and Ochose, protects the entryway of all homes.

Ogun offers you protection in matters relating to surgery and operations, accidents, fevers, and other kinds of wounds inflicted by metal. He enjoys white beans, sweet potatoes (roasted), plantains, smoked fish, kola nuts, palm oil, toasted corn, alcohol, and cigars.

Any offerings made to Ogun are left at railroad tracks because of his affiliation with metals. His prominent syncretized saint is Saint Peter, but he is also affiliated with Saint Michael, Saint Rafael, Saint Paul, and Saint John the Baptist to a lesser extent.

Ogun lives in three-legged metal cauldrons, and his place is usually beside Eleguá. He, Ochosi, Eleguá, and Oshún are called the Guerreros (divine warriors). His eleke is made of interlacing green and black beads.

His Babalawos and santeras often wear metal charm anklets or bracelets with keys, locks, and other metal pieces hanging. This is called an acchabá. Ogun's children are impulsive, violent, and unforgiving. They are also brave, astute, hardworking, determined, and never give up hope. Most people know them for their sincerity and frankness, traits that make people pay less attention to their flaws.

In the biological system, Ogun rules your thorax, which is the symbol of strength and vitality.

Yemaya (Yemojá): The Ruler of the Seas

- Catholic Saint: Our Lady of Regla
- Manifestation: Beautiful Woman in Blue and White Garments
- Day of the week: Saturday
- Associated number: 7
- Color: Blue, White
- Feast Day: September 8
- Animals: Sheep, Rams, Ducks, Roosters, Guinea Hens, and Pigeons
- Taboos: None

Yemaya is the great owner of the sea. She lives in them and rules over them. Water is essential in life. So, without her, it wouldn't be possible to live or exist on Earth. Although she is nurturing and maternal, she is just as fierce. She exerts great punishments when outraged. She also forgives when remorse is shown. She is a fair-minded queen.

Yemaya is brave and clever. She loves her children and even goes to war on their behalf. When she does this, no one can defeat her. She is an expert wielder of the machete. Her beaded necklace comprises interlacing royal blue and crystal beads. It is made in a pattern of seven since that is her number.

Traditionally, she is depicted as wearing a long flowing blue dress with a wide belt and a skirt of blue and white ruffles. It is representative of sea waves. She likes the scent of verbena perfume.

As a religious mother, she is full of wisdom and virtue. She also enjoys dancing and having a good time. When Yemaya dances, she starts slowly and gracefully and eventually increases the speed and intensity to reveal her immense power.

Her children are usually strong-willed and independent women. They know how to get what they want. They are sincere in their care of others and can see things from different perspectives. They love children and are protective of them. One might even describe them as being domestic.

In general, Yemaya's daughters are as calm as the sea and rarely lose their temper. But when they do, it is often terrible. Because they take their roles on Earth seriously, they may come across as a bit arrogant. Like their mother, they are maternal and devoted to children. Yet, they find it difficult to make friends.

In an ilé, Yemaya is placed in a blue-colored flower porcelain sopera with water. She likes seashells, sea horses, nets, anchors, and anything that has to do with the sea. She is also associated with the stars, moon, peacocks, and ducks.

She controls the sea's depths that are accessible to humans. Yet, the ocean's deepest parts belong to another deity called Olokun (the owner of the oceans). Humans cannot go deeper into Olokun's realm because survival isn't assured. Yemaya rules over the part where you find plants, fish, and different consumable marine lives. She is linked to the nurturing and creative forces of the deep sea.

Yemaya is great at divination—she learned by spying on Orula, her husband, behind closed doors. Women weren't allowed to use the epuele (divination chain). Yet, she was good at divining, so much that Orula made a pact to enable her to use the diloggún for divination. That is where the tradition of using cowie shells originated. Santeros and santeras can consult with diloggún but Babalawos use the epuele (divining chain).

According to a pataki, Yemaya was the daughter of Olokun. At different times, she was married to Orula, Obatalá, Babalu Aye, Agayú, Orisha Oko, and in certain legends, Ogún. She is known as the mother (foster) of all the main orishas and the elder sister of Oshún.

She is the patron of all pregnant women and a spiritual mother to all those who feel lonely and lost. She is always available to listen and offers her maternal warmth to those who need a mother.

Oshún (Ochún): Queen of the Rivers

- Catholic Saint: Our Lady of Charity
- Manifestation: Beautiful Woman in Yellow Garment with Gold Trimmings
- Day of the week: Saturday
- Associated number: 5
- Color: Yellow, Amber, Gold
- Feast Day: September 12
- Animals: Pigeons, Hens, Guinea Hens, and Castrated Goats
- Taboos: Generic

According to many of the sacred stories, Oshún is the youngest of all the orishas. After Olodumare finished creating the world, he relaxed and appraised his work. He then realized that two things that would make the Earth worth living on were missing: love and sweetness. So, he created Oshún and sent her down to the world to bless others with those qualities.

Oshún is the ideal feminine goddess. She is the orisha of love and sensuality. She embodies femininity and has a seductive nature. She is the ruler of the rivers. A long time ago, all the waters on Earth belonged to Yemaya, Oshún's older sister.

But one day, while Ogun was chasing Oshún in the fields and forests, she fell into the river and was carried away by the whirlpools. Yemaya rescued her and took her under protection. She also gave her the rivers so that she could rule over her own kingdom. From that point, the rivers became Oshún's, while Yemaya ruled the seas.

Both sisters have a cordial and tight-knit relationship and often work together, particularly in matters concerning marriage, motherhood, and romance. Oshún is in charge of conception. She inspires carnal love and blesses people with fertility. Once she successfully ensures sexual love, Yemaya takes over child-rearing.

Oshún is the most beautiful of the goddesses. You may liken her to fresh flowing water. She is sparkling, vibrant, energetic, and refreshing. She makes people pay attention to her with her seductive laughter, honey lips, and graceful dancing.

She is described as having a lush body with full hips, suggesting eroticism and fertility. Her favorite things are silks, perfumes, mirrors, fans, amber and coral jewelry of all kinds, bracelets, and honey. The sunflower is her favorite flower.

While she is young and is somewhat frivolous, the other orishas respect her because she is super powerful. In different instances, she triumphed over her enemies with her sweetness and feminine wiles.

Her colors are amber, yellow, and gold. She is especially dear to Afro-Cubans because of her syncretism with the Virgin of Caridad de Cobre. Her symbols are the vulture and the peacock.

A pataki narrates that Oshún turned into a peacock and flew to the heavens to inform Olofi about a problem the orishas had on Earth. None of the other deities was brave enough to do this because they knew they would burn to a crisp if they got too close to Olorun.

As she flew closer to the sun, her feathers became charred, and the peacock's beauty became lost. By the time she got to Olofi, the peacock resembled a vulture. Olofi is all-knowing, and he knew what Oshún had done, so he rewarded her by making her one of his favorite orishas.

Oshún and Eleguá have a friendly relationship. He supports her in everything she does. She is Shango's favorite wife, but she isn't dependent on him. She is powerful in her own right, and she has been married to other orishas, including Ogun, Orula, and Ochosi. Due to her past relationship with Orula, she is particularly friendly to his priests, the Babalawos. Most sacred stories point to Obatalá as her father.

Oshún has male and female avatars. Hence, she has both sons and daughters in the religion. Like her, Oshún's children are lively and fun-spirited, and willful. They also tend to be social climbers. When you see a child of Oshún, you can instantly identify them by their yellow adornments.

The goddess of the rivers lives in an amber porcelain soup tureen filled with water from the river. Her eleke contains alternating yellow and amber beads in a pattern of five. Sometimes, a little green or red is added to the design.

She likes honey, yellow rice, oranges, sweets, shrimps, crayfish, spinach, river fish, parsley, chard, sweet potatoes, pumpkin, and squash. She also likes tamales, scrambled eggs, and ochinchin.

Oshún helps people with fertility issues and protects them against medical conditions such as hemorrhages, blood clotting, lower stomach and intestine problems, and others. Several people call her Yalorde, which means queen.

Oyá: The Owner of the Wind

- Catholic Saint: Saint Theresa
- Manifestation: Goddess of the Wind and Storms
- Day of the week: Friday
- Associated number: 9
- Color: Red, Brown
- Feast Day: October 15
- Animals: Pigeons, She-goats, Hens, and Guinea Hens
- Taboos: Rams

Oya Yansa is the goddess of winds and storms. She is the one who brings change into your life, whether wanted or not. Of the female orishas, she is the fiercest. She rides side by side to battles with Shango. Like Shango, she also fights with two swords and lightning.

She is in charge of the realm between the Earth and the other side. One of her duties is to ensure that nobody oversteps the boundaries between life and death. She is a very private person, which is why she likes to wear a mask.

Oya often spends her time with Yewa and Oba, both female orishas who live in the cemetery. But her favorite companion is Shango. The patakis narrate that Oya was Ogun's wife before Shango seduced her and took her away to become his wife.

Shango is infamous for seducing the wives of other male orishas, for which he made many enemies. One night, his enemies captured him while he was dancing at a party and locked him in jail. Then, they threw the key away.

Oya was anxious because he didn't come home, and, in a vision, she saw that he was locked up as a prisoner. She called down a powerful storm and sent a lightning bolt to break down the jail bars where he was being held prisoner. Then, she rode in on the gusts of a storm and rescued him. Since then, Shango respected her as a warrior.

Although he isn't a remarkably faithful husband, he knows not to cross her in battles. Oya has an army made up of egún (the dead). She fights with a violent wind. The patakis say she is the daughter of Obatalá and Yemu. Sometimes, she is called Yansá. Oshún and Yemaya are said to be her sisters.

Oya wears all colors except black. She resides in a sopera with nine different colors or black and brown hues. Her followers wear nine copper bracelets because that is her color. She likes white rice, black-eyed peas, eggplant, and grapes.

Her devotees shake the large framboyan tree's seed pod with sounds that echo thunder to invoke Oya. Some say that the rainbow belongs to her because of her clothing's colors. She is the mother of the marketplace. Any offerings for Oya are left there as a sign of change and transition.

Her followers also wear beaded necklaces made of alternating dark brown and dark red beads, sometimes with yellow stripes. Oya inspires fear in people, but she is also protective of those who respect her. She is the symbol of freshness, as she takes away the things that no longer serve you and commands the wind to blow in new things.

Oya's children are powerful and strong. They are as calm as a breeze when happy and violent when crossed. They are loyal and capable of making good partners. They also show strong feelings of jealousy.

The seven orishas discussed so far are called the seven African powers because they are the most revered, known, and influential orisha. But they are not the only orishas that are worshipped in Santería. Others include:

- Ochosi
- Orula

- Agayú

- Babalu Ayé

- Osun

These are also powerful orishas in their own right. If you decide to become a Santería initiate, you might even get one of them as your patron.

Chapter Four: Cultivating Ashé and Iwa Pele

Ashé is the primordial energy surrounding the universe and everything within it. It permeates the Earth and heavens. Olodumare was the creator of ashé, and Olorun manifests it. Remember that Olorun rules the sky and the sun. Without the sun, life cannot exist. In the same way, life cannot exist without ashé.

Ashé is the most sacred possession of all Lucumí practitioners because it is their only link to the divine presence of Olodumare. It embodies everything: knowledge, wisdom, authority, divine grace, and the experience of those who existed in the past.

It is the life force that dictates the strength, vitality, power, and purpose of humans on Earth. One cannot define or explain ashé in concrete terms because its very nature is metaphysical. No matter how you try to imagine or describe it, the meaning will always exceed the limitations of your mind.

The key is to understand ashé as a spiritual and bodily experience because it is central to your existence on Earth. It is just as crucial to your being as the blood that flows in your veins. Ashé is inside your body, and you carry it around at all times. It is what makes you who you are.

The origin of Ashé dates back to the time before human existence. As clarified, Olodumare, Olofi, and Olorun are all manifestations of God. They are like the Holy Trinity in Christianity. Olodumare is the creator of the universe, Olorun used the vital energy of the Sun to breathe life into it, and Olofi serves as the intermediary between the orishas and God. The orishas, in turn, communicate the wills of heaven to humans.

The orishas were some of the first creations of Olodumare. He required them to spread ashé throughout the universe. God granted the orishas divine powers by embodying them with the Sun's energy.

Before the universe's creation, Olorun was pure energy. The universe was created due to the energy explosion. It was charged with ashé, which made it possible for Olodumare's creations to grow and flourish.

One of the most apparent manifestations of ashé is the Sun's life-giving force. Ashé is accessible to humans through communication and interactions with the orishas. For you to acquire ashé, you must seek the orishas' guidance through prayers and divinations, ceremonies and rituals, offerings, iwa pele (good behavior), and making wise choices. These are also necessary to safeguard the ashé you already possess in your body.

In the Lucumí community, some people are recognized as having "tremendo ashé," which means tremendous ashé. They have a great deal of ashé flowing through their bodies, which allows them to command admiration and respect among other community members.

According to many variations of the creation story, Obatalá is the oldest orisha and Olodumare's first child. He was sent down to ayé (Earth) to become God's representative in this sphere of the universe. Olodumare put him in charge of ashé distribution throughout the continents.

Olodumare is the only one with the power to give life, which happens when Olorun breathes divine breath, emí, into empty human bodies. In an earlier chapter, you learned how Obatalá molded humans with clay and Olorun then gave them life. Well, inadvertently, he breathed his divine energy into us. That is why humans primarily possess some degree of ashé.

We all possess varying amounts of ashé. Some have more than others. One sacred myth says that all knowledge of the world's creation was embedded in a giant pumpkin at one time. The divine being, Ejiogbé Odí, was blessed with the task of carrying the pumpkin. One day, he dropped it, and several pieces landed all over the universe. Wherever a portion of the pumpkin fell became permeated with ashé. It became impossible for it to be concentrated in one place or person.

By nature, humans are the hosts of ashé, but we are not all the same. Therefore, we don't have the same amount or kind of ashé. The degree of ashé you possess is based on your character, behavior, and to an extent, destiny or fate. If you have good character, you can gain more ashé through the orisha. If you don't, you lose what you already have.

One important thing to remember is that all things in the universe possess ashé, so you should never disrespect others who seem different from you. There is no definitive way to know how much ashé another person has because no one truly understands its mysteries.

Iwa means moral character. It defines you as a person. You need iwa to live harmoniously with your ashé. Although there is no concept of sin in this religion, the idea of good and evil exists. Olorun monitors your actions on Earth, and he dishes out ashé according to your behavior.

Olorun put Obatalá in charge of teaching humans moral order and a code of ethics. He tasked him to help us develop iwa rere or iwa pele, good moral character, and ethics on Earth. The requirements are for humans to devote themselves to God, the orishas, and their ancestors, and also to treat other creations of God with respect and reverence. You are expected to be a good parent, child, sibling, community member, and godchild. In other words, when people describe you, they should use the word "good."

Obatalá teaches humans to be calm and always keep a cool head. His teachings encourage us to think and reflect before acting or speaking. According to him, you should strive to be a model character in your community. But this doesn't take away your free will. It is still up to you to choose how you want to live and behave on Earth.

If you choose to use your ashé for immoral and harmful purposes, Eleguá will be there to exert punishment. This is why evil people mostly suffer one or more consequences during their lifetimes. Eleguá strips their ashé away and causes them to live out of harmony with everything around them. They live the path of iwa pele.

He also opens their path to illness, loss, conflictive relationships, premature death, and other misfortunes. In a strict sense, good and bad behavior have no moral judgment attached. However, Lucumí emphasizes the essence of proper living in practical terms. If you develop iwa pele, you will live a fulfilling life. And those who choose to live unethically will ultimately live an unhappy and unfulfilling life.

They will always be troubled by negative thinking and feelings because they deviated from the proper path. Every individual is responsible for their actions because Olodumare and the orishas only help people who help themselves.

Ashé, in its true nature, is neither good nor evil. It is a neutral force, in the same way as an electrical force. It is powerful and can help or hurt people, depending on the iwa of those who wield it.

Santería teaches that good cannot exist without evil, since they are two sides of a coin. For there to be good, there must be bad. Ideally, ashé exists so that humans can lead productive lives. You cannot use ashé to eradicate "bad" from the world or your life. Still, you can use it to ease your life experiences. No matter how hard you try, you cannot live to the ideal. Whether you like it or not, you may stray from the path of iwa pele occasionally. It is all part of the human experience on Earth.

The human head is the home to ashé. Individually, your ashé lives in your orí (head). Its presence there is called Eledá, meaning creator. Orí has both physical and figurative meanings, but most people are only familiar with its literal meaning.

Your ori is your guardian or orisha, who takes care of you at all times. It contains every secret of your destiny on Earth. By accessing it, you can learn about the best ways to live the most fulfilling life.

The concept of destiny in the African traditional religion is complex. In simple terms, everyone chooses their destiny before birth. That means your destiny is written before you come down to Earth. Your ori already knows what you will be and everything about your journey on Earth. Through the crown of your head, you can connect with the divine.

Ashé and Initiation

When you are initiated into the Lucumí, an orisha chooses you. He or she enters your body through your crown, explaining why many refer to the initiation ceremony as "crowning." Many people also call it the seating of the orishas or asiento. When the orisha enters, your ori is strengthened by their presence.

Before initiation, you undergo a ceremony to determine the orisha that rules or "owns" your head. From the period of initiation, the orisha collaborates with your ori to call harmony, peace, stability, and balance into your life.

Without connecting with an orisha first, you cannot access or use ashé. Orishas are the only ones with direct access to ashé since they are Olorun's descendants. Their ashé manifests as mountains, rivers, seas, oceans, wind, volcanos, plants, trees, thunderbolts, and other natural elements.

Once you are fully initiated into regla de ocha, you become the son or daughter (omo/omi) of one orisha. There are two potential ceremonies you may undergo to find out the god that owns your head.

In the first ceremony, you are locked inside an Ifá-centric ile (religious house). Then, an Orula priest (Babalawo) uses cola or palm nuts to draw the Odu (signs) that serves as signals of your head's owner. The second ceremony involves staying in an ocha-centric house where an experienced santero uses cowrie shells (diloggún) to draw Odu on your head for the same purpose.

These two ceremonies are much more than a regular consultation with the gods (consulta), where various orishas can talk to you or try to help with a specific problem. The ceremony to find your mother or father among the orishas only happens once in your lifetime.

Once an orisha claims your head, it means that you have established a lifelong commitment to him or her. For this reason, initiation is not something that you jump straight into. You need to think about it thoroughly and make sure that you are ready for that kind of commitment.

Inside Ifá-centric houses, you can't become an initiate until you have received cofa de Orula or mano. After an orisha claims your head, you might be told that you are now a prisoner of that orisha. Before you traditionally find out the ruler of your head, make sure you have saved enough money for the initiation. Orishas are always excited about crowning new community members, and they don't wait once it is confirmed.

Godchildren with experienced godparents in the religion tend not to hurry with knowing who rules their heads because they don't need to know until making Ocha. Before you do anything, know everything about the orishas and form a good relationship with all of them. After this, you can choose one to devote yourself to.

The orishas are jealous beings, and they don't like it when their children are over-attentive to another of them. For example, suppose your orisha is Yemaya. In that case, she may not appreciate you devoting your time to Oshún, Oya, or any other orisha, for that matter.

That is why the initiation ceremony needs to be performed at the right time and in the right way to make sure the orishas don't misunderstand who owns an individual's head.

An important thing to remember about regla de ocha is that you can't always believe what people tell you. If you go for a consulta, the priest might say that you are the child of a particular orisha. While it is true that the odu that appears during a reading may be associated with one specific orisha, it is not enough information to ascertain that a particular orisha wants to claim your head. Such an orisha might just be trying to help with a problem.

For instance, if the odu of Obatalá appears during a consulta, he may be offering blessings, warnings, or trying to speak on your behalf. It does not mean that he wants to claim your head. It might even be a show of fondness. Over time, the same orisha may be revealed as the owner of your head through the appropriate ceremonies. But make sure you don't jump to a conclusion.

There is a famous saying that goes, "Knowledge is a dangerous thing." This saying has never been more accurate than in the case of the Lucumí religion. Individuals who are new to this religion are often excited or anxious to know their mother or father. Due to this, they try to find shortcuts that end up with them striking an instant bond with one of the orishas.

They may decide that Shango is their father because they love his fiery and passionate nature. Some people hear about Oshún's sweet and sensual nature and immediately decide she's their mother. Once they find an orisha they identify with, they just go ahead and choose that orisha as their head's owner. For example, it is not uncommon to hear people say, "I don't practice Santería, but I am a daughter of Yemaya!"

Most people are drawn to Santería because of the myths and legends, songs and dances, and the orishas themselves. The fact is that these are all superficial reasons. When you decide on your own that this or that orisha is your owner, you claim a purely delusional bond that may later affect you when you get initiated. It is a dangerous thing to do.

Usually, there is nothing wrong with professing love and respect toward the orishas that you identify with. As an aleyo (uninitiated), you can worship all the orishas through songs, prayer, and offerings of fruit, candles, or flowers.

But remember that the orishas are inherently jealous beings. They have certain human qualities that cause them to react to issues in specific ways. They can forgive when they need to help those who reach out to them, but they are also quick to punish those who disrespect them.

Calling yourself the son or daughter of one orisha that may not be the ruler of your head is a form of disrespect to the orisha who owns it, and you may get punished for that. If you aren't careful, playing favorites can get you into trouble with the orisha.

Before working with them in a deep or meaningful way, you must clearly define and structure your relationship with them. But how do you do this?

First of all, you must clarify the cause of your attraction to the religion. There are different times of the year when everyone pays renewed attention to all the orishas. This tends to happen during their feast days. During the special days, every Lucumí celebrates and honors the divine gods and goddesses.

This is also when many newcomers hear about them for the first time and develop a strong attraction to some or all of the orishas. They jump to a conclusion about which orisha they want to be devoted to, with little to no knowledge of the orisha. Sometimes, their experience is inaccurate or limited.

Feelings, dreams, and premonitions may attract you to the orisha, but choosing is not up to you. The orisha chooses you, not the other way around. You can't change or control this. You might be used to making your own choices and getting your way, but this is different. It is usually a humbling experience to find out that you can't make this choice.

Waiting to know your mother or father in the religion can be challenging. But by doing the ceremony at the right time and in the right way, you make sure that your reasons for entering the religion are not superficial. You also honor your ancestors and elders' traditions and show the kind of character expected of children of the orishas.

Do not hurry to claim a bond or relationship that an orisha has not acknowledged. These things take time, which is why patience is considered a virtue.

The Head-Marking Ceremony

The head-marking ceremony is how to discover which orisha owns your head. It is straightforward and can be completed in three easy steps that are detailed below.

The first thing to understand about this ceremony is that an orisha won't just choose you based on your personality. Many people think of Santería like astrology and zodiac signs, whereas there are vast differences.

Although many people tend to have the same traits and characteristics as the orisha that rules their heads, it is not always the case. In West Africa, an entire household can sometimes belong to the same orisha. Still, they can't all have the same personality and traits. So, head-marking barely has anything to do with your character.

Sometimes, the orishas choose you because they represent your innermost needs. Only the orisha that best supports your destiny will claim your head. An orisha is meant to help you achieve balance and stability by aligning with your orí.

So, a hot-headed athlete might need to align with the calm and peace Obatalá radiates to achieve their destiny. From the first glance, a hot-headed person might seem like Ogun's child. Using a more introspective approach, you will find that their patron is another orisha entirely.

Before the head-marking ceremony, you must have chosen a priest or priestess to work with in a religious house. Again, you shouldn't do this ceremony unless you have decided that Lucumí is your path. You can't just walk away after finding out your orisha. The knowledge is often accompanied by an instruction to initiate, which you must follow through to get the spiritual support and guidance you seek.

The head-marking is done in the three ways below:

1. For practitioners with godparents, the diloggún of the godfather or godmother's orisha is used for the head-marking reading. Typically, the godparent gives the cowrie shells of their orisha to another santero or santera to ensure neutrality. The person may be given taboos during the reading, and these usually hold until their initiation. This first head-marking method is typically used in Lucumí households that don't work with Babalawos.

2. Three Babalawos use the sacred palm nuts of Ifá called Ikin to consult Ifá about the orisha who owns a person's head. Sometimes, the Babalawos may be more than three, but they are never less than three. This is done to ensure that the odu marked on the divining tray (Opon) is accurate. Also, it helps to make sure that you receive sufficient information about the meaning, interpretation, lesson, and taboos of the odu. Any taboo you get must be adhered to until you receive the Hand of Ifá (Awofakan/Isefa/Kofa). During this ceremony, you are offered the sacred icon of Ifá or initiated to the orisha of your head. This particular method is used in Santería households where they work with Babalawos regularly.

3. A person may also find out their orisha during ita—a divination ceremony that accompanies the reception of orishas or initiation. It is life-bound until superseded by initiation into the priesthood. When you receive the Ifá's icon, you can find your orisha and other initiations you may need to receive. Again, any taboos that show up are binding until initiation. This particular method is standard with those who practice Isese back in Nigeria. It is also used in Lucumí houses that work with Ifá priests.

You may be encouraged or required to receive Ifá if you decide to use the third head-marking ceremony to determine your religious mother or father.

Cultivating ashé and iwa pele is easy. As you have learned, you need iwa pele to access more ashé. The key to developing iwa pele is to treat God, the orishas, and everyone around you respectfully. That is all. Respect is the most important thing to the orishas, and it is the basis of good character.

Once you learn and apply this in your daily interactions, your ashé multiples and becomes more powerful, but don't forget that you have to be crowned to access the full power of ashé or use it to get the things you want from Olodumare through the orishas.

Chapter Five: Altars and Stones

An altar is a sacred space dedicated to a certain orisha or entity for spiritual and ritual purposes. Altars have existed since the beginning of time and are central to the Lucumí religion. Ultimately, it is a place for meditation, self-contemplation, and prayers.

It is also a place to honor those you love and respect, meaning that it is not only for orishas. In Santería, you can also set up altars for your ancestors. Don't forget that reverence to ancestors is a vital part of the religion.

Setting up an altar is probably the easiest thing to do, as long as you understand the requirements. You don't need to be an advanced santero or santera to set up your altar. It is a personal space for building a solid relationship with your orishas and cultivating your divine energy. It is all about building trust with the world around you.

All orishas have individual requirements for setting their altars. Some items may be sacred to one orisha but taboo to another. And you don't just set up altars for all orishas. Any altar you set up in your ile should be specifically for the orisha that owns your head. After setting it up, proper maintenance is essential to strengthen your relationship with your religious father or mother.

Before proceeding to how you can set up an altar for your orisha correctly, let's talk about otas (stones) because they are just as crucial as altars in Santería.

After wood, stone was the most used natural element in the primitive age. Man built an arsenal of survival from its use, and religious worship even arose over time. At that time, rock was a working instrument through which humans built houses and could take shelter from unfavorable weather. More importantly, the figures of the first orishas were sculpted from rock (or stone).

The rock symbolizes firmness since its solid texture and structure make it the basis of civilization's development of construction. This is, in turn, associated with longevity that correlates to the saying, "If you want something to last, make it of stone."

Otá is the Yoruba term for stone. Through the stone, orishas are represented and identified with certain types and numbers of rocks. The orishas live in stones. You often hear that a particular orisha lives in a stone, but it isn't just any stone.

Each orisha lives in a specific kind of stone. Collecting the stones for your orisha requires different rites and ceremonies. Stones are symbols of the divine powers of the orishas. According to Yoruba legends, they enclose the sacred power of the deities.

Every orisha is different, and this is apparent in the kind of stones they reside in. Their representative colors characterize the rocks they like. In Lucumí, the rocks are collected from rivers. You then consult the oracle to learn which orisha a stone belongs to.

If you consult the oracle and get a positive answer, it means that the stone you choose is suitable for your orisha. This is precisely how it works:

> • You collect stones that have the color of your orisha from a river. Make sure that the number of stones you collect aligns with your orisha's associated number. Then, you wash the

stones with a special mix of herbs and water called omiero. In another ceremony, you ask your orisha if he or she accepts the akuta (lifeless stone) you bring for their worship. If you get a positive response, it becomes a living stone.

After acceptance, the divine energy of the orisha takes refuge in the ota, complementing it. Usually, you have to collect the ota first before determining if it corresponds with your orisha. However, there are places you can search and features to look out for to ensure that you get the exact stone corresponding to your deity.

For example:

- Obatalá: collect stones that are around or at the top of a ceiba tree.
- Shango: stones that are near the sea or at the foot of a palm or ceiba tree.
- Oshún: any stone collected from a river.
- Yemaya: any stone near, around, or from a sea.

When you collect the stone, you must subject it to a purification process to release the negative charge and boost the vital life force. After this, the stone is consecrated and put in the space where you have set up an altar for the deity. The stones are extensions of the gods themselves, so you must accord them with respect and behave appropriately when in their presence.

Stones that are also used in significant Lucumí ceremonies are collected by ordained priests or priestesses. Also, during initiation, the santero confirms that the stones are suitable for the initiates' rebirth.

Now, here are examples of the proper items needed to prepare an altar for each orisha:

Obatalá

To create Obatalá's altar, you need:

- A white cover cloth.
- A metal crown.
- A white Obatalá candle.
- A bell with a dove handle.
- Items for Obatalá Ayaguna.
- Items for Aguida Obatalá.
- A soup tureen of Obatalá's color.
- An Obatalá statue, doll, or relevant image.

Offerings made to him on the altar should include white foods such as meringue, cocoa butter, coconut, white yams. Avoid offering him alcohol, salt, or spicy foods at any time.

Yemaya

To prepare Yemaya's altar, you need:

- Cowrie shells.
- Silver items.
- Fans.
- Pearls.
- Images of sea creatures, such as mermaids, fish, dolphins, waterfowl, and others.
- Blue cover cloth.
- Silver or blue crown.
- A statue, doll, or image of Yemaya.
- A soup tureen of her favorite color.
- Yemaya incense.

- A blue or white candle.

- Blue flowers such as irises. If you cannot find blue flowers, go for a bouquet of different colors.

Offerings to Yemaya may contain all kinds of seafood, fruit, white wine, and coffee.

Ogún

For Ogun's altar, you need the following items:

- All types of metal tools, especially his favorite. Refer back to Chapter Three.

- A complete cauldron set.

- An iron rooster.

- Iron; a cannonball, anvil, or any other iron object.

- An Ogun candle, preferably green, brown, red, or black.

- Nails.

- An image or statue of Ogun.

Ogun offerings should include plantains, pomegranates, grapes, red meat, rum, gin, and cigars.

Eleguá

Set up Eleguá's altar with:

- Toys, marbles, bells, and other child-friendly objects.

- A depiction of crossroads.

- A statue or image of a baby or adult Eleguá.

- A prayer card.

- Eleguá head statue.

- Black and red candles.

- A black and red cover cloth.

Eleguá enjoys offerings of yellow rice, fish, candies, toasted corn, tobacco, and liquor. He also likes palm oil and red pepper.

Shango

Shango's altar should contain:

- A crown.
- Swords.
- A double-headed axe.
- A batea, i.e., lidded wooden bowl.
- A pilon, i.e., pedestal for the bowl.
- Wooden tools.
- Double-headed thunderstones.
- A bata drum.
- An image of Shango.
- A red cover cloth.
- Red candles.

Offerings to Shango should include spicy and fiery foods. He also enjoys all red-colored foods, such as red apples and pomegranates.

Oya

For Oya's altar, use the items below:

- A feminine crown.
- Shea butter.
- Fresh eggplants.
- Multi-colored cover cloth.
- A soup tureen.
- Osun de Oya.

- Copper jewelry.
- A depiction of a lightning bolt.
- Red gourds.
- Rainbow-colored candles.
- An image or statue of Oya herself.

Offerings to Oya should include eggplant, chocolate, purple grapes, beets, and wine. She also enjoys sesame seed candy, black beans, rice, and chickpeas.

Oshún

Here are the essential items for Oshún's altar:
- Yellow or gold cover cloth.
- Sunflowers.
- White and yellow candles.
- An image or statue of Oshún.
- A pot of honey.
- Sensual perfume.
- A sopera i.e. soup tureen.
- One pencil.
- Cinnamon.
- A white bowl filled with river water.

Oshún enjoys offerings that contain her favorite foods such as honey, oranges, yellow rice, squash, pumpkin, eggs, et cetera.

Apart from the orisha altars, there is another type of altar called the Boveda altar. This is the altar you set up for your ancestors in the spiritual realms. Remember that ancestor worship as part of this religion, so this is just as important for you to have in your home.

The Boveda

The boveda altar is a portal for you to connect with your ancestors. Everyone can initiate direct contact with their ancestors in the spiritual realm. Communicating with those of your lineage who have turned to spirits can unravel who you are as you navigate life. Your ancestors can complement the orishas.

There are different ways to connect with those in the spiritual realm, and setting up a boveda altar is just one of those ways. You may also refer to it as an ancestral altar. In the English language, "boveda" literally means tomb or vault.

The ancestral altar is a sacred space for you to give offerings and reverence to your ancestors' spirits. By doing this, you can get their guidance, protection, and clarity. They can even offer you knowledge on how to strengthen your ashé and iwa pele.

You can set up a boveda altar in different ways, but here is how Santería practitioners and Afro-Cuban people generally construct one:

- Technically, you need a small table to set your altar. It should be covered with a white cloth, white candles, fresh flowers, and incense.

- Add one big goblet, or three, seven, or nine small ones. You can choose any of these numbers, but nine is recognized as the number of the dead. It represents death, rebirth, and completion.

- Fill the goblets with cool water and ensure you change them weekly. Also change the water when the goblets become cloudy.

- The water represents clarity, so it must be clear and clean at all times. It also provides purification. The central glass is for your orisha and the rest for your ancestors.

- Place the water glasses in a formation with the largest in the middle, while the rest form a circle around it. Naturally, you can use any other formations you wish.

- Add offerings of sweets, pastry, cigars, alcohol, and other foods to make your ancestors happy.

One of the best ways to solidify your connection with your ancestors is by offering them rituals. You may commit a particular day of the week to them. Cleanliness is of utmost importance in ancestor worship. Make sure the altar is clean at all times. Be as clean as possible whenever you make offerings and prayers.

If you don't know your ancestors, during offering or prayer, simply state that you are calling upon the spirits of your ancestors' good moral characters. Communicate with them as if they are physically in the room with you. Listen for advice, guidance, or instructions.

The Boveda altar should be white with lighting at all times. Freshwater is a necessity because the ancestors lose clarity when the water turns cloudy. Replace flowers regularly, and don't let the food attract bugs before you dispose of it.

Greet your orisha and ancestral altar every morning before you start your day. Also, service them weekly.

These steps are simple and straight to the point. With consistency and devotion, you will get all you wish for from your orisha and ancestors. Just keep honoring those on whose shoulders you stand.

Chapter Six: Cowrie Shells: The Mouths of Gods

In ancient Yorubaland, cowrie shells (diloggún) were of the highest importance. They served different purposes and contained various meanings. Ancient Yorubans used them for buying and selling. They also served as jewelry. A newly-wedded bride is typically adorned in cowrie shells for beautification reasons. Most importantly, the Yoruba used them, and still use them, to communicate with the orishas.

Cowrie shells are the mouths of the gods. The art of cowrie shell divination is an indispensable aspect of the Lucumí religion. The practitioners of this religion rely on the orishas' advice and guidance. They also seek assistance from their ancestors when making decisions or going through hard times.

Cowrie shells are sacred divination tools through which you can interact with your orisha or ancestor. Although divination generally requires comprehensive training and involves some specific procedures, you can still learn to use the diloggún to interact with your spiritual guides.

Santería devotees believe that these sacred shells open up the pathway through which one can access the realm where infinite knowledge and wisdom are stored. Without them, you cannot tap into the timeless view of the ancestral realm.

Some say that the magic of the diloggún comes from its appearance, which can be likened to a half-open eye. Others say that it is connected to femininity. They see it as a symbol of fertility.

Only trained olorishas and Babalawos can do divination because it is a sacred act that requires the use of adequately consecrated divination tools. Priests of Orula and Santeras can only interpret what the orishas say through cowrie shells after following precise training and initiation.

Interpreting the diloggún requires a level of ashé that not many people possess. Everyone wants to learn how to do the reading, but the truth is that you need to be a specialist to accurately read and interpret the cowrie shells.

Each orisha has a particular set of diloggún, but Santería priests and priestesses generally start with Eleguá's diloggún. It can be used for general consultation, since Eleguá can speak for all the other orishas. So, if you want to learn diloggún divination, you may start with his set.

Eleguá's diloggún contains twenty-one shells, but only sixteen of these are used in a reading. The remaining orishas have eighteen cowries in their sets.

In Cuba, the divination ritual is called a consulta, a Spanish word for consultation. Anyone can decide to get a consulta or registro at any time, for any reason. However, most of the time, you should already have preliminary knowledge of Santería and the divination procedure before going for a reading.

Typically, you can divine for guidance and help when you feel anxious or uncertain about a situation. By consulting the orishas, you will determine whether the situation will bring you iré (blessings) or osorbo (challenges/obstacles) based on your decision.

If the orisha brings up osorbo, the diviner can help you determine the origin and cause. The orishas may also proffer a viable solution to remove the obstacle. Usually, the remedy involves making rituals and offerings to whichever orisha can help eliminate the obstacle from your path. If iré shows up during a reading, the diviner may tell you to do certain things so that the blessings stay in your life.

A cowrie shell reading can provide in-depth information about different aspects of your life, including the physical, emotional, personal, professional, and spiritual. It can tell you a lot about your family, friends, career, health, finances, marriage, and other matters.

It may also offer you warnings about envy, insincerity, greed, jealousy, and potential betrayal, which could negatively affect your life. By combining practical advice and metaphysical teachings, cowrie shell readings can help you achieve harmony so that you can live the life you desire and deserve.

If the orishas give a piece of advice and you try your best to adhere to their instructions, they will do everything to ensure your progress on your chosen path. But if you neglect their advice and teachings, your situation may worsen.

Cowrie shells are not the only mouths of the gods. Another form of divination in Santería is obi divination. It is considered the simplest form of divination in Lucumí. The word for coconut is obi, a sacred tool that must be handled with respect.

The procedure is simple. The diviner breaks open a fresh coconut with a mallet or machete. If you want to try this, remember that you cannot break it on the floor. It must remain in your hands as you break it.

After the coconut is split open, you select four parts with equal sizes. If necessary, trim them to get a manageable shape and size. Follow this with the prayer and ritual protocol, then throw the obi pieces to the floor and ask yes/no questions. Generally, obi divination is done to determine the kinds of tribute an orisha wants, where to place it, and if they are satisfied after the offering.

Readings require you to enter with serious intent and a firm commitment to what the orisha has to tell you. Do not do a reading with the idea that an orisha will narrate what the future holds for you. You are the maker of your future.

The orishas can only offer you guidance to ensure you don't stray from your path, but they may never reveal your path to you. With their help, you can create the life you deserve. If there are specific issues you need to resolve, a reading can reveal that to you.

You may even be asked to change specific behaviors or the way you interact with the world. Cowrie shells don't offer a quick fix, but if used the right way, they can set you on the path to personal, professional, and spiritual growth.

Cowrie Shells and Odu

When you throw the diloggún during a reading, they reveal letras, i.e., signs, letters, and patterns known as odu. A diloggún set contains sixteen consecrated cowrie shells. The basic patterns are also sixteen, and they are known as the "parent" odu.

The first throw of the cowrie shell during divination reveals a composite comprising two-parent odu. Diviners call this pattern the entoyale. It gives vital information about the general themes to be addressed during the consultation.

There are 256 possible patterns when you throw a diloggún. How your shells fall determines which composite pattern turns up. Each of these has specific characteristics that you will learn how to interpret in the next chapter.

Suppose you want to be a good diloggún diviner. In that case, you must memorize as much information as you can about each odu pattern. Traditionally, Lucumí practitioners in Cuba don't share the most secret information about odu with non-members of the religion. It is sacred information that is known only by the priests and priestesses of the religion.

Godparents also have the knowledge, but they guard it carefully and choose if, when, and under what circumstances they share this knowledge with their godchildren. Learning the odu isn't something you can achieve in days or months. It requires a massive commitment of time and effort that many practitioners just can't devote to it. That is precisely why only a few initiates master the odu.

It is best to go to a trained specialist if you want to consult with the orishas through the cowrie shells. However, suppose you are serious about Santería, and you can devote enough time to learning. In that case, there is no harm in trying. Just understand that you have to put in years of practice.

Nevertheless, whether you do the training or not, practicing Santería requires you to know the names of the odu, as well as the patakis and proverbs attached to them. Sometimes, pataki offers personified information about an odu, and this also gives valuable insight into the lives of the orishas while they were on Earth.

The odu are primordial beings. They are older than the orishas and share a direct connection with Olofi himself as one of his first creations in the universe. At varying points in time, Olofi sent them down to Earth, where they interacted with orishas and humans. Then, they returned to heaven.

Patakis provide insight into the relationship between the odu and different orishas and why the odu interact with human beings in a specific manner. Folklorists think of odu as archetypes that explain various human conditions. For Santería devotees, they are divine messengers.

Traditionally, santeros and santeras in Cuba only read the first twelve odu. The priests of Orula read the rest. At this point, it is crucial to explain the difference between olorishas and Babalawos.

Regla de Ocha and Regla de Ifá are two closely-knitted religious traditions, both with roots in Yoruba culture. But there are minor differences between them. The latter, which is Regla de Ifá, only allows heterosexual males as initiates. Once fully initiated, they become priests of Orula, otherwise known as Babalawos.

Most initiates in Ifa don't need to make ocha first. They go directly into Ifa worship and skip orisha initiation. Women and males, straight or gay, can receive cofá de Orula and Mano de Orula, respectively.

These are ceremonies for people under Orula's protection and ensure they don't suffer a premature death. Not everyone needs to get Ikofa, but you will be informed during a consultation with a Babalawo if you need to. You don't have to be an Ifa initiate to consult Orula's priest.

What sets Babalawos apart from olorishas is that they are the only ones who know how to channel Orula, the master diviner. Orula knows all the secrets of the world, and he can reveal them to his Babalawos.

With his help, they can guide people toward their destinies and maybe even change or influence their future. Orula oversees everything from birth to death. He knows the exact time that every human being will die.

A trained and skilled priest can use the epuele to channel Orula's knowledge about the most critical issues. Generally, Babalawos don't work with diloggúns for divination purposes. Still, they can work closely with the olorishas or aborishas (non-initiated practitioners belonging to an ile) to interpret any odu that appears in diloggún readings.

It is your choice to make whether to consult with a Babalawo or an olorisha whenever you want the orishas' guidance. To some extent, your choice may be influenced by the level of confidence you have in the Babalawo or olorisha's ashé. So, make sure you choose the right one before a consulta.

How the Odu Guide Us

The odu are categorized into two classes: major and minor odu. These reflect the order in which they came down to Earth. Unle is the eldest odu, and Oché is the youngest. The hierarchy of odu influences how you interpret any information that shows in the diloggún.

When a santera divines with the cowrie shells, the reading can come with either of two things: ire or osorbo. Ire means blessings and good fortune, whereas osorbo means obstacles and misfortune.

You can determine a reading orientation using ibó which can be anything from a stone to a chalk (efún) or a bone piece. The person (priest) doing the reading hands over the ibó to the subject, who rubs it gently in his or her fists. Then, he or she separates both, with one left in each hand.

The priest instructs you to remain fisted to avoid knowing the contents of both hands. Then, he casts the diloggún, which brings forth an odu. Beforehand, he must have learned the odu's hierarchy to discern between the major and minor odu.

To determine which of your hands to examine, the diviner needs to have learned the odu's precise ages. This is important for him to ascertain seniority and hierarchy. The odu which appears will tell the diviner which of your hands to examine. Then, the ibó tells him whether the reading is ire or osorbu.

The priest's first step is to figure out the source of the orientation, be it ire or osorbo. Usually, ire is easy to interpret because it can only take a single form (good fortune). But it can have varying sources from the orishas to eleda and other entities.

Osorbo's interpretation, on the other hand, tends to be more complex and multilayered because it takes different forms from tragedy to loss, witchcraft, sickness, et cetera. The sources also vary from orishas to ancestors, family members, eleda, friends, enemies, et cetera.

Diviners need more time to accurately interpret readings with misfortunate orientations because they require as much information as the odu can give.

How Santería Perceives Adversity

Naturally, most people want good fortune readings. But priests believe that readings of misfortune (osorbo) help people better than anything. They believe that adversity and misfortune are vital for personal growth and character development.

People embrace growth when they have problems that need solutions. Adversity and misfortune provide an opening for you to learn important life lessons.

Sometimes, when people are constantly and consistently blessed with ire, they become vague and overconfident in their abilities. This pushes them to neglect the roles that the orishas play in their fortunes because they believe there's a guarantee. It also tends to push them toward self-destructive mistakes and choices.

The good thing is that ire and osorbo are transient. They are not here to stay forever. If anything, both conditions are the orishas' way of gauging ashé and deciding whether it is time to give people a spiritual boost or not. Ire and osorbo let you know your spiritual standing with the orishas and your ancestors.

If you get a reading with osorbo orientation, you only need to work with a trained santera to figure out its source and make amendments. Doing this eliminates the problem from your life. Most of the time, one only needs to carry out a sacrifice or other offering (ebbó) to get the solution. Further divination will tell you the exact kind of offerings the gods want.

Sometimes, the orishas ask for behavior modification, especially if you behave in ways that displease them. Other times, they simply tell you the specific steps to take to correct the problem. Osorbo isn't an indicator of eternal misfortune and tragedy. It is more an opportunity for you to fix the problems you didn't know you had in your life.

As mentioned before, the orishas never help the people who don't help themselves. For them to help, you must be taking active steps to show them you are worthy of their help. This religion is an interactive one, which means that you must work closely with the orishas to resolve your problems. If you don't make an effort, they will simply sit back and watch everything unfold.

Osorbo can be remedied through taboos that last for a short period. The priest cannot impose permanent restrictions, but he or she may tell you, for example, "Avoid the public and large crowds," "Never answer the door once you've retired to bed at night," or "Don't share your business plans with anybody."

These temporary restrictions are meant to shield you from potentially dangerous situations relating to the odu you get during a reading. By avoiding situations where osorbo can potentially manifest, you can avert the misfortune shown in the odu. Sometimes, you don't have to experience misfortune before you remedy it. As long as you listen to the guidance from the orisha during a diloggún reading, you will be fine.

The next chapter delves into actual divination and how to read and interpret the odu.

Chapter Seven: Biague and Cowrie Shells: Divination

The biague and the diloggún are the two prominent oracles used for divination in Santeriá. Through them, one obtains the gods' opinions, advice, and help. They also help by counseling and healing. One by one, let's discuss how both oracles are used for divination.

Obi Divination (Biague)

The previous chapter gave a brief insight into the art of coconut (obi) divination. Here, we will dive deeper into the practice. Obi is also referred to as "Biague," in honor of the first priest to use Olodumare's divination gift. According to one pataki, Olodumare visited the Earth and was enchanted by the beauty of the coconut palm, so much so that he blessed it with a gift.

Olodumare told the palm it would be more than a source of nourishment and oil to humans. He blessed it so that the orishas could read the future from its fruit. "Your fruits shall bear meanings to the Orishas, and they shall pass them on to men."

Obi divination involves interpreting the positions of obi pieces thrown on the floor. As you've learned, the coconut only responds to yes/no questions. So, you can only ask direct and straightforward questions. For example:

"Should I marry the man I just met?"

This question may receive any of the answers below:

- Alafia: Yes, you may.
- Ocanasode: No.
- Eyife: Definitely.
- Otawe: Unsure. Throw the obis again.

The simpler your question, the easier the interpretation of the biague. Obis are pieces of a broken coconut shell. Their oracular power comes from ashé, which is vital to communication between orishas and santeros.

When divining with the biague, ensure you ask one question of each orisha at a time. As a beginner, Eleguá is the only orisha you should try invoking through the coconut shells. You may use the biague for daily consultations, but you don't have the liberty to repeat questions.

If you start repeating questions, Eleguá may become bored and start playing pranks on you. He may intentionally give odd and upsetting responses to your questions. Note that stupid questions are an insult to the orishas. They are neither to be used as a source of amusement or as party games. You might be punished if you don't treat them with respect.

Even if you aren't an initiate, you can consult the gods through the biague. Again, you only need to accord them respect. The prayers and invocations for opening should be made in the Lucumí language because that is what the gods prefer. But they also understand all languages, so feel free to try English or any other language, as long as you do it in your own words.

How to Consult the Coconut Shells

Find two gourds and place them in your divination area. Note that you cannot use faucet water. Fill one with fresh water from the river, and fill the second with a mixture of the following items:

- A pinch of roasted corn.
- Smoked fish or hutia (jutia, large rodent).
- One spoonful of honey or molasses.
- One smear of corojo butter.
- Powdered eggshells.

Place a candle of Eleguá's favorite color(s) in the area. In this case, use a red and black candle. If you are consulting a different orisha, the candle should be of their favorite colors.

- Choose a coconut and strip it of its outer husk until the nut comes free. Split the nut into different pieces with a hard object, e.g., a machete or hammer. As you know, the coconut must not be broken on the floor. Note that coconut milk will pour out from the inside; allow it.

- After breaking, choose four clean coconut pieces without cracks or any imperfections. They will be your obi for divining. Wash them in the fresh river water you kept in one of the gourds.

- Hold the obi in your left hand, then use the right one to pick out coconut meat bits from all the pieces' corners. The number of pinches should match the consulting orisha's number. For Eleguá, you are to pinch three times.

As you pick out the coconut meat pieces, chant:

"Obí ikú obí ano obí eyo obí ofo ariku babagwa."

- Light the candle in honor of Eleguá. If you have his image or statue around, place the candle before it. Otherwise, place it by your front door.

- Place the bits you pinched off the obi on top of his tureen or a small plate beside the lit candle.

- Carry the gourd that contains the mixture and include witch hazel leaves or Sargasso. Pour in some of the river water until it forms a thick composition. Put the gourd beside the candle and call upon Eleguá to take the coconut meat pieces as his offering.

- Sprinkle the river water around the offering three times as you chant: "Omi tutu ana tutu laroye tutu ilé."

Take the gourd with the mixture and spill a little in all the corners of the room you are in. Drop some outside your front door to protect yourself against osorbo. In case something unfavorable comes up, the cleansing ritual can help you change the outcome.

Once you are done cleansing and purifying the room, pray to Eleguá in your own words. The good thing is that you can compose your prayer to beseech Eleguá to open up the pathway to the other orishas.

The prayer is called mayubo, a form of greetings to the orishas. Below is the mayubo for Eleguá:

- "Laroye akiloye aguro tente onú apagura akama sees areletuse abamula omubata okoloofofo okolonini toni kan ofo omoro agun oyona alayiki agó"

If you cannot understand and pronounce the above prayer accurately, just compose a prayer in your own language.

After summoning Eleguá through the opening prayers, pay respect to Olodumare, the dead, and the spirits of your ancestors. Finally, seek the permission of your godparent to throw the obi. It does not matter that they aren't physically present. They are there with you spiritually.

- Place the four obis in your right hand, even if it isn't your dominant hand. Gently touch the floor and the orisha's sopera with your left hand and offer a greeting. Repeat "Ilé mokueo

Eleguá mo kueo" three times. If there is someone else there with you, they should reply with "Akue ye."

• Next, dip your left fingers in the spilled water on the floor. Then, moisten your right fingers with your wet, left fingers.

• Throw the obi on the floor as you chant: "oni ele bake."

These are the preliminary steps to consulting the gods through obi. Next, you have to interpret their positions on the floor to determine the answer. Here are possible permutations from the thrown obi.

Alafia

Position: The four obis land with the white part facing up.

Meaning: Affirmative.

Interpretation: Everything is right and proper. Happiness. Health. Grace. Peace and prosperity.

When you get an affirmative position, bow before the obi and show reverence to the orisha. Repeat your question and toss the obi. Eyife or Otawe must follow Alafia.

Eyife

Position: Two obis land white up. Two white down.

Meaning: Yes.

Interpretation: Definitely. Affirmative. Absolutely. Positive.

If you previously threw Alafia, the answer is a definite yes. You don't have to throw again.

Otawe

Positions: Three white sides up. One down.

Meaning: Uncertain. Maybe. Doubtful.

Interpretation: What you asked is possible, based on certain conditions—no complete confidence.

When you get otawe, throw the obi again. This time, be as specific as possible with the question. Toss again, and you will get a definite answer. If you get another otawe, the answer is no.

If you previously had Alafia, you may need to carry out a sacrifice. Further consultation with the oracle will pinpoint the exact type of sacrifice to be offered.

Ocanasode

Positions: One white side up. Three shell sides up.

Meaning: No.

Interpretation: The answer is negative. Be alert to avert misfortune. Beware of tragic occurrences—grave challenges.

When you get this, throw the obi again and ask specifically if it means plain "No" or if there are complications and difficulties.

Oyekun

Positions: All four shell sides are up.

Meaning: Death. Loss.

Interpretation: A sign of terrible things to come, particularly death and suffering.

When you get oyekun, place the four obis into the gourd with water and add eight cocoa butter pieces. Doing this refreshes the obi from negativity. As the obi are soaking in water, touch your chest and do a prayer to ward off death and suffering. Then, touch the floor and do the same.

Immediately after your consultation, go to a Babalawo immediately. You will be given a despojo ritual cleansing to ward off evil powers and influences. Go to your ancestral altar and light a candle for the spirits of the dead.

Cowrie Shell Divination (Diloggún)

The orishas talk through the openings of the cowrie shells. They are not usable for divination until you have cleanly filed the domed sides to make what looks like a hollow shell. But don't touch the side where the opening is because the gods will speak through this. First of all, you have to make your oracle. Since you can easily buy the shells online in stores where they sell Santería items, the next step is to make sure they are suitable for divination.

As mentioned before, a set of shells contains eighteen cowries. Of these, only file sixteen of them. Set the remaining two aside without touching them. These two are meant to be diloggún's guardians, and they are called edelé. Then, add a tiny black stone to the sixteen filed shells and one eggshell piece for handling the diloggún during reading. Finally, add a small piece of bone. Once you do this with your cowrie shell set, you are ready to start divining.

As the diviner, you must hold the black stone in your left hand and the eggshell in your right. According to the odu that appears, which will either be left or right-handed, ask Eleguá a question for the objects in your hands.

If you get the black stone, that odu is negative. And if you get the eggshell, the odu is positive. A positive reading comes in ire, while a negative reading comes in osorbo. The implications of both have been explained in the previous chapter.

As noted, the odu are divided into major and minor ones.

- **Major odu:** 1, 2, 3, 4, 8, 10, 12, 13, 14, 15, and 16.
- **Minor odu:** 5, 6, 7, 9, and 11.

The following are the possible outcomes of a single odu throw:

1 - Okana (one mouth up).

2 - Eyioso or Eyi Oko (two mouths up).

3 - Ogundá (three mouths up).

4 - Iroso (four mouths up).

5 - Oché (five mouths up).

6 - Obara (six mouths up).

7 - Odí (seven mouths up).

8 - Eyeunle or Unle (eight mouths up).

9 - Osá (nine mouths up).

10 - Ofún or Ofún Mafun (ten mouths up).

11 - Ojuani (eleven mouths up).

12 - Eyilá (twelve mouths up).

13 - Metanla (thirteen mouths up).

14 - Merinla (fourteen mouths up).

15 - Marunla (fifteen mouths up).

16 - Merindilogún (sixteen mouths up).

Opira is the seventeenth possibility, which is when no mouth turns up. It indicates that there is a significant problem with the consultation. It may be on the part of the diviner or the individual seeking clarification from the orishas.

Because many of the Lucumí teachings were transmitted through oral tradition, there are variations in spellings.

The placement of odu tells you whether it is left or right-handed. The reading is in the left hand when you get the major odu, all double numbers, and: 6-7, 6-5, 6-9, 9-7, 11-9, 9-5, 1-5, 7-5, 8-9, 3-7, 12-6, 11-5, 10-11, 4-11, 11-6, 1-2, 2-5, 1-6, 1-5, and 10-6.

The right hand is when you get the minor odu and: 11-10, 7-6, 11-1, 5-9, 11-3, 5-12, 5-6, 6-12, 5-7, and 9-12.

When consulting the gods through the diloggún, you throw the major odu once and the minor ones twice. If you get a minor odu, throw it again. But generally, you should always repeat the first throw regardless of whether you get a major or minor odu.

The Meanings of Odu

- **One Mouth Up:** This is related to creativity, beginnings, independence, leadership, willpower, originality, and isolation. It gives answers about aspects of oneself.

- **Two Mouths Up:** Gives answers about relationships. It is associated with harmony, partnership, duality, division, solidarity, tolerance, and balance.

- **Three Mouths Up:** Related to family. It has to do with fertility, family, energy, abundance, fulfillment, and self-expression.

- **Four Mouths Up:** Associated with the community. Tells you about dedication, reality, order, stability, manifestation, dependability, strength, and truth.

- **Five Mouths Up:** Tells you about your life's purpose. Associated with communication, curiosity, knowledge, freedom, travel, restlessness, search, logic, and change.

- **Six Mouths Up:** Gives answers about aspects of service. Linked to beauty, perfection, love, devotion, fidelity, duty, balance, sympathy, wholeness, and service.

- **Seven Mouths Up:** Tells you about spirituality. Associated with introspection, religion, faith, and the ethereal. The message might be from your ancestors.

- **Eight Mouths Up:** Linked to personal achievement, strength, accomplishment, power, confidence, and success.

- **Nine Mouths Up:** Associated with the divine, compassion, generosity, selflessness, humanitarianism, healing power, and charity.

- **Ten Mouths Up:** Gives answers about personal projects. Associated with endeavors, struggle, luck, health, prayers, delayed achievements. It may also mean that the orishas want you to become a Santería initiate.

- **Eleven Mouths Up:** Answer is associated with negativity. Related to tragedy, loss, negativity, direction, control, and the evil eye.

- **Twelve Mouths Up:** Indicates a coming war. Associated with privacy, respect, friends, temper, and visiting. May mean that you shouldn't go out in public and keep your affairs private.

- **Thirteen Mouths Up:** Related to health, disease, illness, menstruation, throat, blood, et cetera. Requires you to see a Babalawo immediately.

After determining your reading outcome, you may need to ask more questions to get specific answers or adequately interpret what the orishas are telling you. Consider starting with yes or no questions to get answers that are easy to interpret.

The diloggún can reveal vital information to you and offer insights into your future through the odu. If you wish to connect with the power of odu, try keeping some shells in your pockets or wallet. Cowrie shells are said to be a magnet of financial success. You may also throw them into a moving water body while you make a wish.

In the tiny little shells, you can find protection, blessings, wealth, and fertility. You only need to ask the orishas and do whatever they request of you. The diloggún and obi are prized treasures of the Yoruba ancestors. Their children (and others) continue to benefit from them today.

Chapter Eight: Ebbó Rituals and Sacrifice

Ebbó is the Yoruba word for offerings, rituals, and sacrifices to the orishas and spirits. It is central to many African traditional religions, including Santeriá. Both humans and orishas require ashé to navigate life. One of the ways to increase your ashé is by making offerings to the orishas. Sometimes, you may carry out ebbó just to show respect and admiration to the gods.

Animal sacrifices are considered the most effective type of ebbó because the orishas enjoy meat and blood from their favorite animals. Refer back to Chapter Two for the misconceptions surrounding animal sacrifice in Santería.

There are various kinds of ebbó apart from animal sacrifice. For example, you may pledge not to eat certain foods, do a specific action, or engage in some activities. These are also offerings to the orishas. Others include burning candles or offering fruit and flowers at the orisha's altar. Singing, drumming, and dancing are other forms of offerings that orishas receive.

Apart from these minor offerings, there are major rituals and sacrifices that a devotee is sometimes required to do to ward off evil, or boost ire. Usually, the orishas tell you the kind of ebbó they want during a consultation.

These are the kinds of ebbó they may ask for:

• **Ebbó Idupe/Lope/Ope:** This is an offering of gratitude to the orishas or a particular orisha that has blessed or helped you. The point of this ebbó is to show awareness and thank a deity for his or her blessings. It may also be to fulfill a promise made to the orishas on the condition that they give you a specific blessing.

• **Ebbó Idanewan:** Also called iyeyun, this ebbó is given as an act of charity. The purpose is typically to feed the community or perform some other act of kindness. In some cases, it is done to feed the representative of an orisha or anybody under their guardianship. A good example is feeding animals that are sacred to the orishas or watering their favorite plants. Lucumí devotees believe that you feed the gods themselves when you feed their children. In places where animal sacrifice isn't allowed, this is one of the ways you can give offerings to the gods and your ancestors.

• **Ebbó Sisun:** Translates to "burnt offering." Ebbó sisun is given to fire-oriented orishas such as Shango and Aganju. You may add meat, special woods, and aromatic materials to the offering. Also, ensure you compose poems and offer praise to show your appreciation. Ebbó sisun can also be offered in the form of fireworks.

• **Ebbó Misi:** This is an offering you give by making liquids that are sacred to the orishas or an orisha you seek bodily contact with. Basically, you prepare the liquids, consecrate them, dedicate them to the orisha, and then apply them to your body. Some are for healing and cleansing, while others are used to glorify or adulate an orisha. You can also spill the liquid around your altar area.

- **Ebbó Tito:** Used to right a wrong or appease an orisha. Ebbó tito is the offering to give when you go against an orisha's instructions or do something that is tabooed. In that case, you carry it out together with ebbó iyeyun to compensate for any damage.

- **Ebbó Ti Abo:** In the English language, abo means protection. So, this offering is made to court the protection or guardianship of any orisha. It can help if you are in a profession with potential dangers. Also, it is an offering for those who need spiritual, psychic, and physical shielding from harm.

There are several other kinds of ebbós, but these are the most popular ones. You can do an ebbó privately or publicly, depending on what the orishas request of you. But if the ebbó falls during celebration holidays, you can make it public to get ashé flowing throughout your community. Of course, this depends on whether you are in a Santería-friendly community or not.

Some ebbós require you to be an initiate of the religion. Others require you to be a first-generation member of the community. But in general, you can be supervised by an initiate or santera.

Some deities are less or more humane than others. A more humane orisha is typically more challenging to deal with. You need a high degree of ashé to communicate with them. They may become angered if they feel disrespected or offended.

So, as a newcomer, it is best to offer ebbó under the supervision of an experienced priest. Otherwise, you may need to avoid them altogether. The good thing is that anyone can do ebbó iyeyun at any time. The orishas love it when you feed their children.

If you can't go to the crossroads to offer ebbó to Eleguá, just feed a young child, an old man, or someone that is a known child of Eleguá. You may also offer them gifts. If you can't carry ebbó to the river for Oshún, give away some money, jewelry, perfume, or other lovely things to one of her children.

Taking care of children and old people is an excellent way of adulating Eleguá. Beautifying yourself to appear prettier glorifies Oshún. Getting your hands dirty with honest work adulates Ogun. Cleaning the beach makes Yemaya happy.

Suppose you can't be as spiritually active as the orishas demand. In that case, you can make donations to a priest or practitioner that doesn't mind making the sacrifice on your behalf.

The Orishas, Herbs, and Ornaments

Every orisha has a group of magical, healing herbs. Some are specific to a particular orisha, while others can be used for all the orishas. The herbs are usually put in the omiero (spiritual water) used to wash the orishas' stones.

One of the most common recourses for Santería followers is taking a herb bath when faced with a problem that does not require animal sacrifice or ebbó in general. Usually, you should have a gourd in your home that contains your orisha's favorite herbs and fresh water from a river.

You can use herbs for physical and spiritual cleansing. Not only can you apply them to your body, but you can also cleanse your house with them. Some can even be consumed for internal cleansing. Herbs are the easiest and cheapest method for solving problems and getting rid of evil forces in your life.

When you need to do a herb cleansing for different orishas at once, make sure you pile each group of herbs separately until you are ready to mix them in the omiero. Do this to avoid mixing them up before it is time to mix them.

Depending on the orisha you worship, you can wash your hands in their omiero to improve your health or purify yourself.

To prepare omiero and herbs, you need a deep mortar or sopera that belongs to the orisha you are consulting. Do not boil the herbs, but know that you can't use dry leaves. You may wash the orisha stones as frequently as needed until the orisha you want is invoked. As you wash the stones, offer greetings and prayers to the orisha. Once you have cleaned the stones, no animal sacrifice is required.

The seven main orishas discussed earlier have their favorite ornaments, which you should consider adorning during the herb bath and cleansing.

Obatalá

- **Herbs:** Chamise, Amansa Guapo, almonds, goosefoot, white hamelia, white peonies, calla lilies, Madonna lilies, sweet soursop, yucca, witch hazel, sweet balm, San Diego Blanco, cotton, white elderberry, sweet basil, wild mint, marjoram, blite, jimsonweed, purslane, African bayonet, and eguere egun.

- **Ornaments:** Obatalá's image should be made from silver or white metal. He should hold a crown in one hand. Then, a sun, a moon, a walking stick, four wristlets, a clenched fist, a coiled snake, and a half-moon. All of these objects should be made of white metal or silver. Add two ivory eggs.

- **Eleke:** Made of twenty-one pure white beads, twenty white beads, and one coral bead to reach the desired length.

Eleguá

- **Herbs:** Cuban spurge, wild convolvulus, nettles, abre camino, black-eyed peas, foxtail, manyroot, neat's tongue, crowfoot, jack bean, chili peppers, cordia collocea, ateje, mastic tree, white pine nuts, Sargasso, Bunchosia media, pigeon peas, camphor leaves, heliotrope, coconut husk, peppergrass, corn stalks, corn silk, corn leaves, mint, bitter bush, corojo, avocado leaves and roots, coconut palm stem, cowhage, coffee, wild croton, dried rose, soapberry tree, senna, and many others.

- **Ornaments:** Stone-made statue with cowrie shell eyes, kites, toys, marbles, garabato, crooked cub.

- **Eleke:** Three red beads, three black beads in an alternating sequence. After the first three black beads, alternate the red bead with a black one. Repeat the sequence until you achieve the desired length.

Shango

- **Herbs:** Cordoban, kapok tree, clematis, cashew, arabo rojo, vacabuey, mugwort, Cuban spurge, bran, ironwood, poplar, suguaraya Banya tree, leeks, American spurge, plantains, bananas, bull's testicles, clematis, sorghum, red hamelias, pitahaya, pine, royal palm, amansa guapo, apple tree leaves, pine nuts, lignum vitae, and several others.

- **Ornaments:** Cedar-made machete, axe, sword, dagger, and spear.

- **Eleke:** Six red beads, six white beads, followed by alternating white and red beads in six patterns. Sequence to be repeated until the desired length is achieved.

Ogun

- **Herbs:** Palo bomba, palo vencedor, sasparilla, restharrow, boneset, blessed thistle, carpenter ants, senna, datura, sweet soursop, black pepper, guamoa, mastic tree, castor oil leaves, oak leaves, indigo plant, red pepper, cat's claw, and eucalyptus, among several others.

- **Ornaments:** Iron pot, twenty-one iron pieces, an arrow, a pickaxe, an anvil, a machete, a key, a hammer, and Corojo butter.

• **Eleke:** Seven green beads and seven black ones, followed by alternating green and black beads seven times. Pattern to be repeated until the desired length is achieved.

Oshún

• **Herbs:** Sunflowers, rose, frescura, paraguita morada, hierba fina (fine grass), ale, female fern, purslane, Indian lotus, river weeds, seaweed, anise flower, amber, orange leaves, papaya, marigold, peppergrass, vervain, plantain, lantana, maidenhair fern, wild lettuce, rosemary, creeping crowfoot, mazorquilla, arabito, alambrilla, and cucaracha (cockroach plant).

• **Ornaments:** Copper jewelry, golden crown, oars, bracelets, peacock feathers, rays, spears, arrows, and a bell.

• **Eleke:** Five amber beads, five coral beads, followed by five alternating amber and coral beads.

Yemaya

• **Herbs:** Yellow mombin, cucaracha, chinzosa, water hyacinth, anamu, indigo, Bermuda grass, sponges, seaweed, Florida grass, purple basil, chayote fruit, green pepper, coralline, majagua linden (sea hibiscus), and saltwater rushes.

• **Ornaments:** An anchor, a half-moon, a sun, a key, a siren, a ray, a shovelhead, seashell, and conch shell, all made of lead.

• **Eleke:** Seven alternating crystal and blue beads. The sequence is repeated until you obtain the desired length.

Oya

- **Herbs:** Bonita, marigold, Jamaican rosewood, cypress, aralia, mugwort, camphor leaves, mimosa, espanta muerto, varia, cabo de hacha, peppercress, breakax, revienta caballo (sticky nightshade), and flamboyan tree.

- **Ornaments:** A crown with nine points and nine charms, a shovel, scythe, a gourd, a hoe, a pick, an axe, a rake, a hatchet, and a hoe. Red gourd, lovely copper bracelets, and a lightning bolt.

- **Eleke:** Nine black beads, nine white beads, followed by alternating black and white beads nine times. Or brown, maroon, or lilac beads, striped in multiple colors.

Chapter Nine: Lucumí Rituals and Ceremonies

Initiation into the Lucumí religion signifies death and rebirth. The moment you begin the week-long process, you die and are reborn, symbolically. It means that your old life has ended, and you have begun a new one. The initiation ceremony lasts a week, while the entire process lasts a year.

During this period, a new initiate is referred to as iyawo. As explained before, iyawo means "bride of the orishas." However, a more accurate meaning is "novice." It is a word used for newly-initiated people because they are just entering into a commitment to the orisha. Regardless of gender, all new initiates are iyawos. The year-long initiation process is called iyaboraje.

In an earlier chapter, we discussed the initiation process briefly. This time, we will dig deeper into the rituals and practices involved in crowning a new initiate.

Your first year as an initiate is for purification and rejuvenation. It's a period when you are prohibited from certain foods, behaviors, styles of clothing, and other life aspects. During this time, you interact with and establish intimacy with the orishas.

Traditionally, a new initiate is never referred to by their name during iyaboraje. Instead, they are known only by iyawo to prevent and ward off negative energy and potential osorbo sent by evil people who want to diminish the new initiate's spiritual power.

The use of iyawo is also a way of separating the initiate from their old life to usher them into the new life. In the community, they will likely be given a Lucumí name. New initiates are generally restricted to activities that can't be avoided, such as school or work.

A sacred ceremony called Ita is done during this period. It is a complex and multilayered series of diloggún consultations with different orishas. An oriate and a team of skilled santeros and santeras will interpret what the orishas say through the shells to let you know your new life path.

In Cuba, this is called el juicio final, meaning final judgment, because it gives you a window into your past, present, and future. Whatever information is attained through the cowrie shells, the afeosita (community scribe) writes everything down in a libreta (notebook) dedicated to you. For the rest of your life, you are to consult that notebook when you need to make crucial decisions that could affect your life path.

In general, it offers information about past problems, present challenges, future obstacles, potential health problems, warnings, and the need for behavior modification. It also tells you how to accomplish your purpose and achieve fulfillment in life.

Any prohibition or limitation that comes up during this ritual is binding for the rest of your life. While some may not seem reasonable to you initially, you have to accept and respect them to show that you are obedient and devoted to the orishas. After all, that is the bottom line of your initiation into Santería.

New initiates must learn to accept the orishas' advice and opinions without question. Life is full of mysteries that the ordinary human mind cannot understand. Often, humans don't understand the conditions life imposes on us.

After the end of iyaboraje, another special ritual is done to mark your transition to santero or santera. Upon the end of this ceremony, you can now participate in all Santería ceremonies, feasts, and rituals as an ordained priest or priestess.

The point of the iyaboraje is to evaluate your faith and dedication to the orishas. The initiation ceremony marks the beginning of a serious commitment to Santería. Most Santerías end up putting their "normal" life on the back burner to aid their spiritual growth and development.

Most of the rituals and ceremonies are done inside igbodu, a sacred room for that exact purpose. Typically, a new initiate has to buy new towels, sheets, clothes, and other necessities, which must all be white.

Drumming and Dance

Many outsiders assume that drumming and dancing are for entertainment in Santería, which is wrong. Contrary to the misconception, both are part of the religious rituals done during initiation and the orishas' holidays.

Drumming and dancing are meant to entice the orishas to come down among the practitioners and interact with them through possession. A drumming ceremony is called a Tambor. During this ceremony, the principal instruments are the sacred bata drums: three hourglass-shaped drums with two heads each. These drums are rested across the drummer's lap horizontally and require both hands.

Before a ritual, the bata drums are ceremoniously prepared and consecrated with the spirit of Ana. They can only be used for religious reasons because they are holy and sacred. Like the diloggún and biague, they help the children of the orishas communicate with their fathers and mothers.

The drummers go through intensive training and preparation before they can beat the drums. Not everyone qualifies for this. In traditional Cuban societies, only men are allowed to play the drums.

Iya is the largest bata drum. It is called the mother drum since it is the leader of the set. The iya drum calls changes in songs and rhythms during a ceremony. The second is itotele, the middle-sized drum. Together with the iya drum, this one creates complex rhythms that speak to the orishas.

If you are unfamiliar with the complexities of Yoruba-style drumming, the complexity of the rhythms can be astounding. The drummers use the drums to recreate the language of the Yoruba people in tonal sounds. Those familiar with them can hear and understand whatever the drums say to the orishas in the native language.

As you have learned, okpawon is the name of the lead singer that sings alongside the drummers. Think of this person as the master of ceremonies because they lead the assembled in the call and response to songs.

Before a ritual ceremony, the people in charge of drumming and singing must have established the order of songs and rhythms. Each song is dedicated to a particular orisha or spirit of ancestors, known as egun.

The opening toque (beat) begins with drumming, no singing or dancing. It is called the oro seco. When it ends, the drummers start beating the orishas' rhythms individually until they call them all.

The orisha drumming is customarily opened with Eleguá, since he is the bridge between the world and the other orishas. According to the order of seniority, the priests and priestesses do a salutation (foribale) in front of the drums. It is a formal gesture that involves prostrating flat or kneeling in front of the drums for seconds.

Then, they salute all of the drums by touching their head to them individually. They start with the iya drum and end with the okonkolo, which is the smallest. Lucumí devotees take seniority seriously, especially during the rituals' dancing segments. The eldest santeros are closest to the bata drums. During an elder santero or santera's birthday, a Tambor can also be held in their honor. On occasions like this, the priests can dance near the drums.

As the rhythm increases and songs advance, santeros formally salute the orishas' children, whose song is playing, in the same order of seniority. For example, when Eleguá's song is playing, everyone will salute the eldest child, which is the person with most years in the community, and continue until they reach the youngest. The same goes for all the other orishas.

To some extent, this requires you to be reasonably familiar with community members and greeting protocols. How salutations are used varies from one religious house to the next. So, you need the guidance of a community elder to know how things are typically done. If you are wrong, you will be instantly corrected. Even though the atmosphere is festive, elders demand that traditions and protocols be respected and followed with discipline.

Some traditional Santería communities only allow fully-initiated santeros to dance in front of the drums. But before then, they must have been formally introduced to them. During your initiation, you can dance in front of the drums.

There are dress codes for men and women during these ceremonies. Male initiates who want to dance in front of the drums wear long pants, dress shirts, and caps. On the other hand, females may wear a long skirt, decent blouse, and a scarf for their heads.

They may dress fully in white or wear the colors of their respective orishas. Black is prohibited because it is a beacon for negative energies.

Participants must wear their orishas' beaded necklace, bracelets, and other jewelry that is considered sacred. Note that the eleke and other sacred jewelry are not worn to bed or during sexual intercourse. Always place yours on the altar when you aren't doing anything that requires you to have them on.

For your initiation, you are to hold a Tambor and bear all the cost. The number of invitees determines the cost.

Musical Rituals

Musical rituals follow a secret formula for communicating with the orishas. In Santería, these rituals are called oro or oru, the Yoruba word for "conversation." It emphasizes Lucumí's belief that music and dancing are ways of interacting with the gods.

There are various types of oro to communicate with orishas. One type is pure singing in Yoruba-style call and response, without drumming or dancing. The akpawon (lead singer) chants out to the group, and they respond in unison. The song's function is to pray to the orishas and request their permission to proceed with the ritual or ceremony.

Another type of oro is called the oro del igbodú, which is unaccompanied by bata drumming. Its purpose is to invite the orishas to participate in the ritual. These two musical rituals are held privately inside the sacred room. They are not open to the uninitiated.

The third type of oro is the oro del eya aranla, a combination of singing, drumming, and dancing. This one is open to everyone, including outsiders who wish to participate in the ceremony outside the sacred room's margins.

It lasts for hours and typically attracts a teeming crowd. It is held in the largest space available in the religious house, but participants spill into the streets. The drummers and singers remain within the confines of the ile while performing for the divine deities.

Once the formal song order ends, singing and drumming can become more informal as the drums repeat the rhythms called out by the lead singer. The rhythms are typically accompanied by a gong and a large achere loosely covered with a string of beads (shekeres).

These two instruments cover the empty spaces between the drum beats. Although musical rituals are festive occasions, they start and end on a solemn note to respect the deities and ancestors.

Formal ceremonies, such as the orishas' holy days, are executed with the consecrated bata drums. On the other hand, non-consecrated drums are played at informal gatherings and parties. Informal liturgies are called bembe in Lucumí.

Other Lucumí ceremonies are:

- Divination readings.
- Spiritual cleansing and healing.
- Honoring events for godparents.
- Orishas' anniversaries, which are held on their holy days.
- Funeral rites.

Trance and Possession

It is not uncommon for musical liturgies in Santería to result in trance possession by the initiates in the congregation. Within the community, trance possession is of the utmost importance because it is an avenue for the practitioners to speak directly with the deities.

Possession happens when an orisha mounts an available human body, also known as a Caballo, to interact with the ceremony participants. Santeros allow the orishas to own and possess their body for the benefit of their whole religious community. They willingly put themselves in a state of susceptible consciousness so that the orisha can speak through them.

Trance possession is a legitimate phenomenon for devotees, so they don't care whether outsiders believe in them or not. They also know that some people can fake possession, so they have ways of determining when it is authentic and when it is not.

At one point or another, members of different religious houses have experienced actual possessions where the orishas manifest in human forms and speak to the people directly. A possessed person usually doesn't recollect the event and is unable to converse with the orisha. That is why possessions can only occur in a sacred and shared space or ceremony, where everyone can witness and remember the orisha's visit.

General members of the religious community are in tune with everything that happens in a ceremony. They can recognize when one of the initiates is entering into a trance. They often form a crowd around the possessed individual, chanting, dancing, and encouraging the orisha to mount the body.

The outward appearance of a trance possession is typically traumatic, sometimes violent. The possessed falls to the floor and begins to shake, or runs around the room in an unconscious state. Most of the time, an orisha mounts one of his or her children's bodies when the rhythm in honor of that orisha is playing.

For example, during Oshún's toque, she may possess one of her daughters or sons. During a musical liturgy, multiple people may be mounted at once by different orishas. Once it is clear that an orisha has mounted an initiate's body, he or she is transferred from the room and draped in ceremonial garb representative of the orisha possessing him or her.

Orishas can inhabit the body of anybody, whether male or female. A female possessed by a male orisha will immediately take on the traits of that orisha. For example, someone possessed by Shango might start talking boastfully or walking with a swagger. Such a female is dressed in the deity's clothing.

The same is true for males possessed by female orishas. They immediately take on feminine traits, start dancing seductively and interacting with feminine grace. Once the orishas mount a human body, they join the ceremony to dance, talk, eat, drink, and be merry. They also take the opportunity to give advice and bless their followers.

From an outsider's perspective, the ceremony may appear to be nothing more than an ordinary party. But, in reality, it is a religious experience for the participants and everyone present.

What happens during a trance possession?

The above is a question that outsiders and newcomers often seek an answer to. If you think of your body in biological terms only, you may find it challenging to comprehend how trance possession occurs. But those who are deeply familiar with Santería practices understand that the host's soul temporarily departs their body to make room for the visiting orisha.

They consider this a form of sacrifice since the host is giving up their consciousness for a period to benefit the whole community. The orishas use that period to heal and bless people. They offer an intervention that can make a difference in some people's lives. They also boost the ashé surrounding that community of people.

Devotees consider possessions a positive and welcome experience. They report experiencing profound feelings of joy, love, and peace while hosting the orishas. At the end of the ceremony, the hosts return to a conscious state feeling exhausted and spent.

When the orisha leaves, religious members form a ring around the host body to ensure they don't suffer physical harm or injury. After departure, they carry the possessed into another room to rest and redress them in their original attire.

Not every santera gets to be a host for the gods. Many never experience the gift of possession in their lifetime. It may be because they aren't willing to surrender their consciousness or because the orisha does not choose them.

Suppose that an uninitiated present at a ceremony feels a trance possession about to happen. In that case, the person is taken away from the scene, away from the music, and encouraged to take charge of their consciousness.

Non-initiates are prevented from hosting the orishas because their ashé is too weak to withstand the orisha. Practitioners generally don't allow photos and videos while someone is in a trance.

Holy Days Celebrations

The holy days are the feast days associated with the saints that each orisha is syncretized with. In the chapter about the orishas, you can find the dates for celebrating all the orishas' feast days. Depending on which orisha owns your head, you are required to hold a feast on their saint's day. The feast is simple. All you need to do is give an offering of their favorite things in their favorite number at the altar.

For example, let's say you are a child of Oshún. In that case, you can celebrate her by giving an offering that includes the following items:

- Five pumpkins or squash.
- Five sunflowers.
- A lovely, sensual perfume.
- Yellow candles.
- Five pieces of gold jewelry.

- Honey.

- A bowl of her favorite foods and fruits.

You can follow this for all the orishas as well. On the feast day, place the offering at the orisha's altar. Since holy days are different from every other normal day, ensure that there is a significant difference in the level of offering you give.

Chapter Ten: Lucumí Spells

Spells are an intricate part of Santeriá. They are sacred and are meant to help you get what you want from the orishas. They can be used for different purposes as well. This chapter will teach you effective Lucumí spells that can make personal, professional, and spiritual differences in your life and path.

Spell 1: Feeding the Eledá (Head)

Ingredients:

- Coconut
- Cocoa butter
- Powdered eggshells
- Smoked jutia and fish (Eleguá)
- Black-eyed peas and slugs
- Tamales (Obatalá)
- Two white plates (new)
- Two white candles
- A white handkerchief

Feed the jutia and the tamales to Eleguá and Obatalá, respectively. Then, form a paste from the remaining ingredients. Plate both candles at the center of the white places and light them. Take off your shoes and sit in the lotus position. Hold onto your knees as you sit.

Place the paste around the lit candles on the plates. Hold each plate in one hand and touch the offering to your forehead, shoulders, chest, palms, knees, and feet. Chant a prayer to bless your eleda as you do this. Then, apply the paste to your head. While still wet, apply the white cotton to the paste. Cover your head with a handkerchief and allow the paste to dry.

This spell is used to feed your ori so that it can bring you good fortune and tidings. You should make it a regular practice for your eleda to constantly remain blessed. If you want, you can help other people bless their heads. But don't do this until you are well-versed in practice.

Spell 2: Strengthening the Eleda

Ingredients:

- Four white doves
- Two coconuts
- Cocoa butter
- Powdered eggshell
- Smoked fish
- Cotton
- Corn pepper
- A yard of white cloth

Sit as in the first spell for feeding the eleda. Tear the (already humanely killed) dove's head and let the blood drip onto your head. Make a mixture of the food ingredients until it forms a paste. Then, cover your head with the paste and plaster the cotton onto it. Wrap the white cloth around your head. Cook the doves in a new pot and eat them. Don't forget to chant prayers for your eleda while doing that. In the next three days, keep the mixture and white cloth on. You may not step into the sun, go out of your house, get angry, speak to people, or sleep on any bed for as long as this spell lasts. After the third day, you can take off the turban and wash off the paste from your head with cool water.

This spell helps to make your eleda stronger, so that evil forces and ill-intentioned people don't get access to you or your ashé. It is a powerful spell that should be a regular part of your routine.

Spell 3: Clearing Your Mind and Improving Thinking

Ingredients:

- Powdered eggshell
- Cotton
- Cocoa butter
- Coconut (grated)
- Yam (grated)
- Coconut
- Water
- A large white cloth

If you are dealing with anxiety and unclear thoughts, this spell can help you clear your mind. Form a paste with the grated coconut and yam. Then, mix in the remaining ingredients and soak the cotton with the result. Wrap up the cotton inside the white cloth. Then, lie down and place the cloth on your forehead. Keep your eyes closed for 60 minutes and add coconut water intermittently to keep the mixture wet. After an hour, wash off your head with cool water. You should feel improved clarity immediately.

Spell 4: Removing Evil Eye

There are two spells here. The first one is to remove the evil eye from a young child, and the second is to remove the evil eye cast by a neighbor.

Ingredients:

- Holy water
- Sweet basil
- A white handkerchief

If you suspect that your child or another child is sick due to an evil eye from someone, take the child to bed and let him or her rest. Gently pray to Yemaya over the child and ask for her intervention. Then, take a sprig of sweet basil and dip it into omiero (holy water) until it's moist. Use the moistened sprig to cross every part of the child's body, from the head to the chest, stomach, knees, legs, and hands. When you have finished, wrap the basil inside the white handkerchief and get rid of it far away from your vicinity.

To remove the evil eye that comes from a neighbor, you don't need to do much. Just get a large bunch of bananas and tie a red cloth or ribbon around it. Hang the tied bananas from your house roof until they become rotten. They will have absorbed all the negative energy and envy from your neighbor.

Spell 5: Improving Your Life

Ingredients:

- A red cloth
- Red ribbon
- A white cloth
- A piece of steak
- Corojo butter

- Dried corn

- Powdered eggshells

- Six cowrie shells

- Six coconut pieces

- Six silver coins

- One red rooster

Put the piece of steak on the red cloth. Rub Corojo butter all over it and add the powdered eggshell. Pick up the steak and rub it over every part of your body while naked. When you are done, return it to the red cloth. Wear a white and red dress. Add the corn, shells, coins, and coconut to the steak. Wrap the red piece of cloth and everything inside it on the white cloth. Securely tie up the bundle with the red ribbon. Then, carry the bundle to the foot of a kapok tree and make it an offering to Shango.

Before you put the package down, go around the tree six times as you touch it with your right hand and pray to Shango to grant you a better life. After making the final turn, drop the package at the tree's foot and return to your home. Wait for six days, and then go back to the tree. Sacrifice the red rooster and drop it with the package. This time, make sure you don't touch the tree.

That should be the last time you do a ceremony of any kind at that particular tree. Wait for a long time before you ever go back there.

Spell 6: Removing an Enemy's Curse

Ingredients:

- Banana leaves

- A red piece of cloth

- A red rooster

- Six red apples

- Six red lianas

Go to a palm tree's base. Strip off all your clothes until you are naked. Using the red cloth, wipe all parts of your body. Then, spread the cloth out on the ground. One by one, rub your whole body with each of the remaining ingredients. Pile on the cloth until you have gone through all ingredients. Finally, wipe your body down with the rooster. Tear off its head and allow the blood to drip onto the pile on the ground. Add the rooster's feathers to the bundle and tie everything together. Bury the package at the foot of the tree and leave. Do not return to the tree or that vicinity for a long time. Take the rooster's body home, make a meal with it, and eat. Don't share the food with any other person.

Spell 7: Eliminating Accident Proneness

This spell is usually done to ask Ogun for protection against accidents. If you are constantly on the road, this is one you might want to do regularly.

Ingredients:

- A black cloth
- Eight black roosters' legs
- White chalk
- Owl feathers
- Seven candles
- Rose
- Apple roots
- Shark's tooth
- Mule's tooth
- A large iron cauldron or pot

Use the chalk to draw a cross on the four corners of the black cloth. Then, line the pot or cauldron's inside with it. Light the candles and arrange them inside the pot. Toss in the eight legs of the black roosters, the apple roots, the rose, and the remaining ingredients. Ensure that the owl feathers are enough to start a well-lit fire. As the ingredients burn, ask the orishas to relieve you of your proneness to accidents. Ask Ogun especially. Chant a prayer that is targeted at him. When the ingredients have all burned, carry the pot of ashes to any cemetery near you and bury the whole pot and the contents. Return to your house and say a prayer of thanks to Ogun and the orishas for hearing your pleas. Remember to chant a prayer to Eleguá first.

Spell 8: Petitioning the Orishas

Ingredients:

- Corojo oil
- Almond oil
- Coconut wine
- Iron filings
- Orange water
- Cocoa butter
- Peppercorns
- Mercury
- Red ocher

Get a tin can. Fill it with the almond and Corojo oils, then add seven drops of wine and seven drops of orange water. Add seven bits of coconut meat, seven peppercorns, and one pinch of solid ingredients. Add a wick to the mixture. Go to a nearby seashore and ask the orishas, particularly Yemaya, to come to your rescue. Light the wick, and next to it, place a glass of water with mercury and cocoa butter. Return to your home.

To petition Oshún:

- A large achere
- Honey
- Five eggs
- Oil
- Cotton wicks
- One sugar plum

Punch a small hole in the five eggs and put them inside the gourd (achere). Through the holes, fill oil drops into the eggs, add drops of honey and a bit of sugar plum. Add a cotton wick to each egg. Light the wicks as you chant prayers to Oshún. Allow the lamps to burn for five days. And on the final day, carry the gourd and the burnt eggs to a nearby river for disposal.

Spell 9: Finding the Source of Osorba

When someone sends osorba or a curse your way, this spell can help you figure out who the person is.

Ingredients:

- Transparent glass of wine
- A white candle
- Coconut oil
- Water
- Corojo butter

Choose a quiet room in your house. Go into this room and place the wine glass on your floor. Fill it with water, add some drops of coconut oil and a little bit of Corojo butter. Put the candle next to the wine glass and light it up. Make sure the candle is the only source of light in that room.

Sit in a lotus position away from the glass. You should be at least two feet away. Then, invoke your orisha if you already know which one is yours. Otherwise, invoke Eleguá. Stare at the glass for some time.

Breathe deeply and evenly as you stare. You will likely fall asleep. If you do, the answer will come to you in a dream. If you don't fall asleep, you will see the face of that person in your peripheral vision as you stare at the glass.

This spell and its process requires you to be patient and persevering because it might take a while for anything to show up. You may even see unrelated things in the glass before the real person appears.

Spell 10: Purifying Your Body and Soul

Ingredients:

- Yellow roses
- White roses
- Red roses
- Sunflowers
- Violet water
- Pompeii cologne
- Mint oil
- Chamomile
- Coconut oil
- Rosewater
- Holy water
- Mint leaves

Place the five sunflowers in a big container. Add all of the white, red, and yellow roses, the cologne bottle, five drops of coconut oil, violet water, and five drops of mint oil. Add a bottle of rose water, five handfuls of mint leaves, five handfuls of chamomiles, and five drops of the holy water. Then, pour in five liters of water. Allow the mixture to soak and steep for a full day. Bathe with it before you go to bed, and don't dry yourself.

Here is another spell for purification.

Ingredients:

- Seawater
- Florida grass
- Anamu
- Watermelon seeds
- Witch hazel
- Mugwort
- Marjoram
- Purple basil
- Seven candles
- Seven empty gallons

Go to the seashore with all the ingredients above. Fill the gallons halfway with seawater. Drop seven watermelon seeds into each bottle. Add seven sprigs of each herb. Drop the bottles into the sea for seven hours. Then, one by one, remove a bottle and use it for bathing until you use up all the bottles. Start the bathing ritual on a Saturday. On the final day, light the seven candles and offer them to Yemaya.

Santería practitioners use some of these spells to petition the orishas and ask for their blessings or help. Keep in mind that if you want to start using the spells and rituals of Lucumí, you must be ready to commit yourself to the religion. If not, you shouldn't play around with the spells or try them without the supervision of a trained Santero.

If you are serious about learning Santería's practices, finding a trained priest to teach and nurture you is the best step you can take.

Conclusion

Congratulations on making it to the end of *Santería: The Ultimate Guide to Lucumí Spells, Rituals, Orishas, and Practices, Along with the History of How Yoruba Lived on in America*. Hopefully, you have learned a lot about Santería's religious practices. With the information in this book, you are on the right path to mastering the secret ways of the orisha. To reiterate, Santería is an initiatory religion. Therefore, you should consider this book as a general introductory guide to the religion. If you would like to learn more deeply about the spiritual practices of Santería initiates, you are advised to find a highly-qualified priest to train you in the ways of the orishas. Good luck!

Part 2: Orishas

The Ultimate Guide to African Orisha Deities and Their Presence in Yoruba, Santeria, Voodoo, and Hoodoo, Along with an Explanation of Diloggun Divination

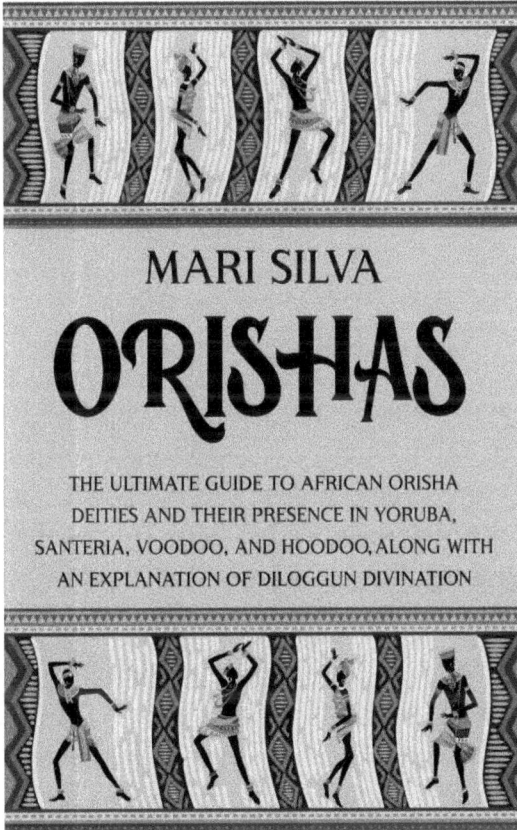

Introduction

We're all connected by nature. From shielding ourselves from the rain to searching for a cool breeze when the weather is hot, we all are influenced by Mother Nature and her offspring. But there's more.

Beyond the influence of cold and heat, daylight and darkness influence the supernatural - the unseen realm and forces therein. While our eyes and natural senses help us see and interact with all that is around us, it requires a special form of awakening to perceive the forces of the supernatural. Needless to say, the supernatural holds a great deal of influence over our lives.

Often, we experience things we cannot explain. For some, it's an unexplainable source of constant good luck, but for others, it could be bad luck over and over. Moments of déjà vu, uneasiness, strokes of luck, or sudden, unexplained fear all find their roots in the unseen forces around us. Although we cannot see these forces, we can feel their impact. These forces are none other than the Orishas.

The Orishas are supernatural forces that influence the course of a person's life. Although they're particularly worshipped in the Yoruba religion, they exist and are greatly celebrated in other religions outside the shores of Africa. Religions like Lucumi,

Candomble, Santeria, among others, all worship the Orishas for their power - the ability to either bring positive or negative influence into the lives of anyone they please. For instance, Orisha Sango is worshipped for his fierce ability to bring instant judgment to an erring person. He is also worshipped to instill courage into fearful hearts. In the same vein, Orunmila is worshipped to draw wisdom into one's life. Female Orishas like Orisha Osun, Yemoja, Oba, Aje, and Oya are also worshipped alongside their male counterparts. Virtually all the female Orishas are attributed to water elements and help female fertility, childbirth, and women's overall beauty.

While devotees of each Orisha have special knowledge on how to worship the Orishas, it doesn't mean that non-devotees are left out. Non-devotees can also learn the ways of worshipping the Orishas, using the basic applicable steps. This means you need not be a core devotee to worship an Orisha of your choice. You need not have all the mystical knowledge about the Orishas before you can pay homage to or invoke their influence in your life.

The supernatural is limitless, and so are Orishas - they are powerful and uncountable. And they are all available and willing to influence your life if you're willing to call upon them. The choice is yours, and this book is here to guide you. In this book, you'll find truths about the Orishas and also the basic steps you need to take to worship the Orisha of your choice - particularly the major Orishas. One thing is certain, Orisha worship is bound to influence your life greatly, and you determine the energy (positive or negative) you draw from them. May you enjoy your fascinating journey with the Orishas!

Chapter 1: How to Worship the Orishas

A Chinese, a Japanese, and a Korean person may look alike, but they're very different. In their beliefs, languages, and manner of interaction, you can easily determine who is who. While it is said, at times, that these three are distant cousins, it doesn't change the fact that they're different. Just as their languages are different (although often claimed to sound relatively alike), their beliefs are different. In the same vein, while the pantheon gods and goddesses of the Chinese, Japanese and Korean people may possess certain similarities, there are clear differences. Culture determines their identity and manner of interaction.

The Earth is home to diverse people and cultures. Each culture comes with its own beliefs that greatly influence how its people live and interact with others. For instance, a Yoruba man is required by culture to lie face down when greeting an elder. But this is not tenable in other cultures where some are required to kneel, bow, stand a distance away, and pay homage to an elder before approaching him. In all of these instances, culture proves its hold on people's lives.

Regarding culture influencing the way and manner in which its people live, an aspect of culture holds greater influence over the people. This aspect serves as the foundation of all cultural beliefs and is known as the belief in the supernatural. Faith in unseen forces often ensures that the status quo in a particular culture is not tampered with. It is easier for a person of culture to explain away phenomenal occurrences and dictate moral principles based on his/her faith in the unseen forces of his/her culture. For instance, a Yoruba elder would explain the flashes of lightning on a stormy night as the works of Orisha Sango, accompanied by his powerhouse of a wife - Orisha Oya. Likewise, a Yoruba person would be wary of doing certain things forbidden by a supernatural entity. All these serve as the basis for cultural and social interactions.

In the Yoruba culture, supernatural forces abound in their uncountable numbers and are classified as Orishas. These Orishas are greatly worshipped by many, and in return, their virtues and powers are drawn into their worshippers' lives. But who are these Orishas?

How Orishas Came to Be

The beginning of the Orishas is deeply rooted in the Yoruba version of creation. While it is believed in most cultural contexts that all of creation came about due to creation by a Supreme Being or God the Supreme Creator, the Yoruba culture thinks a little differently. It is believed that all of creation was carried out by Obatala, a subordinate of the Supreme Being - Olodumare. Rather than Olodumare carrying out the task, Obatala sought permission from Olodumare and was ultimately granted the task.

According to the Yoruba creation tale, Olodumare, also known as Olorun - the Lord of the Skies - had created two separate spaces, i.e., the skies above and the water below – there was no middle or solid ground. With these two spaces created, Olorun (whose name loosely translates to "the head or chief of heaven") took charge of the sky realm above, while his counterpart Olokun (whose name loosely translates to "the head or chief of the deep waters") controlled the water realm beneath the skies.

Obatala was inspired by a need to create a middle ground - a habitable space for creatures to live in. Hence, he sought permission from Olorun to create a habitable space. Olorun understood what was requested and granted Obatala the permission he sought. But there was more needed.

For creation to take place, wisdom was required. Obatala, who is perceived both as a son and a subordinate of Olorun, went ahead to his elder brother Orunmila (the eldest son of Olorun) for counsel. Orunmila, who doubled as the Orisha of wisdom, prophecies, and divination, responded positively and thought about what would be required to create the habitable space Obatala had in mind. By his powers of wisdom and divination, Orunmila stated that Obatala would require the longest gold chain ever for him to reach the surface of the waters below the sky realm. Aside from the golden chain, Obatala would need to fill a snail's shell with sand from the sky realm, which would serve as the foundation for solid ground. Obatala was also required to go with a white hen, a black cat, and a palm nut - all were to be carried in his bag as he made his descent downward.

Having received counsel from Orunmila, Obatala sought the aid of his fellow divinities - sons and daughters of Olorun, and they responded by offering their gold to him. The collected gold was fashioned into a long chain, while Orunmila supplied the remaining items needed for the downward sojourn. With these items in his bag and the chain fixed to a portion of the sky, Obatala made his descent down the golden chain.

Although the chain was the longest ever created, it could not get to the water's surface. Once Obatala had reached the end of the golden chain and realized there was still a lot more distance to go, he prayed to Orunmila. Orunmila responded by instructing him to pour out the sand from the snail's shell and then release the white hen. Obatala did as he was told. He poured out the divine sand and released the white hen. The white hen landed on the poured sand and began scratching - an act that caused the sand to spread out to different areas. Wherever the sand landed, it turned into dry land with certain spots possessing bigger piles of sand that turned into mountains and hills, while certain other spots with less sand turned into valleys.

Having created dry land, Obatala dropped to one of the hills created and named it Ife, which would eternally be known as the "heart of creation" by the Yoruba people. Obatala moved further and took the divine palm nut out of his bag, and planted it. Once the palm nut touched the ground, it sprouted into a full tree and dropped more palm nuts that sprouted with equal speed. The process of sprouting quickly and dropping new seeds that sprouted quickly continued until the whole area was covered in palm trees and new vegetation. Obatala had succeeded in his mission to create a habitable space.

Settling down from the whole creative process, Obatala dwelt in Ife for a while with the black cat as his sole companion. Over time, he grew weary of being alone and, because of this, he devised a plan. Obatala created clay figures that looked like him and that possessed his physical features. Once these were created, Obatala prayed to his father - Olorun, who breathed on the clay figures, and they became the first living men and women of the Yoruba race.

But, there was an error. While creating men and women out of clay, Obatala took a short rest and got drunk on palm wine. With his eyes still unclear, he continued forging more figures of clay. His drunkenness resulted in the creation of many deformed beings – who also became living humans when Olorun breathed life over them all at once.

Once Obatala realized his error, he made an oath never to drink again and always to protect those who were deformed. Because of this, he is also known as the patron Orisha and protector of all with one form of deformity or another.

Please note that while this is the central creation story according to the Yoruba culture, varying tales are similar. In one tale, Obatala needed to fashion a human companion named Oduduwa who assisted in creation. In another tale, Oduduwa is perceived as being the person who carried out the task of creation after Olorun had blessed him. In all these tales, however, Oduduwa remains the father of the Yoruba people, while Obatala remains the widely celebrated Orisha of creation.

Moving on, with the Yoruba race created, the men and women built huts as they had seen Obatala do, and over time the community prospered. This prosperity drew the attention of fellow divinities - gods who came down to visit and interact with the people. Their visits, interaction, and assistance to the people, eventually had them deified by the people Obatala had created. Summarily, the term 'Orisha' was coined to signify their divine status and capacity to help or influence human lives. Obatala and his fellow divinities were sons and daughters of Olorun - they possessed unique powers and virtues sourced from Olodumare and dwelt eternally in the sky realm.

Consequent to their new name, given by the created humans of the Yoruba race, "Orishas" are deified beings, gods, and divinities worshiped by humans due to their divine qualities and abilities to influence and determine the course of existence, not just for humans but for all of creation. For those who yielded to their counsel and instruction, they offered peace and direction. But for those who did not, they were exposed to terrors that could otherwise be warded off by these Orishas. However, they were willing to embrace any who turned to them for guidance.

Classes of Orisha

According to the Yoruba culture, different Orishas manifest in diverse forms but are unified based on their display of power. To know who Orishas are, the first element to look at is the display of power and how much influence such a being possesses. When displaying power, it is well known for an Orisha to show control over an element of nature viz-a-viz fire, water, earth, air, and other elemental forms such as thunder, lightning, iron, and plants. What's more is that each Orisha is capable of divination, can communicate with other Orishas, and has access to powers that are inaccessible to mere mortals. Based on this, it is easy to understand why Obatala and fellow divinities were known as Orishas.

Going through the pages of Yoruba history and culture, certain people were deified and given the name 'Orisha' without actually being of divine origin like Obatala. These were mostly humans who were either the reincarnation of a preexisting Orisha or were blessed by Olodumare and deified by fellow humans based on their extraordinary exploits. They were capable of divination and possessed divine powers, which they utilized to execute unimaginable feats. As such, they were known as Orishas in their own right.

Because power is a major way to identify an Orisha, for any being or human to be classified as an Orisha, such a being or person must possess extraordinary abilities. Mere hunters and people of divination cannot be deified, largely because they have access to measures of power; such powers are mostly based on self-interest. What's more, such powers are often deemed not powerful enough to be reckoned with by the whole Yoruba community. Hence there is no point in classifying such a person as an Orisha – a custodian of power.

The Yoruba culture, just like every other culture in the world, celebrates people of power and sacrifice. Hence, for a person to be deified, they must possess tremendous power and must have used it for the Yoruba people's good. Sacrifice is a hallmark of an Orisha, and, as such, no mere mortal can be deified without having proven him/herself by power and selfless sacrifice for the good of the Yoruba race.

However, here are the classes of Orisha in the Yoruba culture:

First-Class Orisha

The first-class or category of Orisha is beings of divine origin, e.g., Obatala. They were known as Ara orun - the people of the heavens (skies) - because they came from the sky realm and influenced the Yoruba people and their existence. These were sons and daughters of Olodumare, who was the first and supreme lord over all Orishas. They existed before creation, had access to a limitless supply of power, and could appear in human form.

Some say that this class of Orisha initially visited the Earth regularly in their human forms to interact with Obatala's creation. But over time, they returned to the sky realm and ceased their frequent visits to the Earth. To maintain their influence and help those who called on them, they operated via mortal channels such as dedicated priests, graven images, and certain natural phenomena. Orishas in this class include but are not limited to Olodumare, Orunmila, Obatala, Obaluaye, Esu, and Osanyin.

Natural Elements and Other Spiritual Entities

Another class of Orishas is divine beings with tremendous power but who do not possess human forms. These mostly operate via natural elements and phenomenon and are often deemed subordinates or messengers of Orishas' first class. They are known as Irunmole and only operate on the Earth for a specific purpose and time. Once their mission is accomplished, they return to Olodumare.

In a certain respect, Obatala and his fellow divinities were considered to be Irunmole due to these reasons:

- They're subordinates of Olodumare and often serve as his messengers.

- They returned to the sky realm after their Earthly sojourn and have never visited the Earth since then.

- Due to the vacuum created by their absence on Earth, they maintain their operations and influence on the Earth by oracles, priests, and supernatural phenomena.

The Yoruba culture is rife with major and minor Orishas. The major Orishas are widely known and worshiped in the Yoruba culture, while the minor Orishas are not as widely known or worshiped. Minor Orishas who make up this class are innumerable and are strictly worshiped by a select group of people. Often, they're known as Orisha Idile - household gods, and, as a result, only direct descendants of the family worship them. Their followers are in no way restricted from paying homage or worshipping other Orishas - especially the major or first-class Orishas.

One way, as stated earlier, by which this class of Orishas operates is via natural elements or phenomena. Thus, it is believed in the Yoruba culture that there is a spirit behind every natural element or phenomenon. Hence, prayers must be made when a phenomenon is witnessed, or there is an unnatural stirring of a natural element, e.g., prayers are made during thunderstorms to praise or appease the Orisha behind such a manifestation to avoid destruction. Places where unnatural occurrences are witnessed are turned into sacred grounds that must be respected.

Deified Mortals

The next class of Orishas comprises strictly deified humans. Men, women, kings, warriors, hunters, healers who possessed great powers that influenced the existence of the Yoruba race were granted the divine status of Orisha by their followers and the general

Yoruba community as a means of drawing on their virtues and remembering them, despite their departure from the physical/human realm. People like Arabambi Sango were famous kings who were deified by their followers and ultimately became Orishas.

Note, not all powerful mortals are deified. Sacrifice, power, exploits, and overall impact on the Yoruba race determine if a mortal will eventually be deified. Arabambi Sango, for instance, was the fiercest king of the Yoruba people, and he was known for his military and supernatural might. He was known far and wide as the reincarnation of Orisha Sango, the god of thunder, lightning, and fire. This was due to his supernatural ability to breathe fire and summon lightning even without rainfall thunderstorms. Sango ruled with fear and reverence in the hearts of both enemies and subjects alike and was ultimately deified by his followers after his supernatural departure from Earth.

In this same class of Orisha, there are humans just like Arabambi Sango who are known as Orisha due to them being marked by divinities. These reincarnations often serve as channels of expression for the first-class Orishas who no longer visit nor walk the surface of the Earth. They possessed powers and traits akin to the Orisha that marked them and are ultimately worshipped as Orishas in their own right.

How to Worship the Orishas

Before doing anything else, knowledge and an understanding of worship are required. That's the basis for the history and classification of the Orishas. It takes knowing them and how they came about to understand certain truths about them. The truth remains that the Orishas are supernatural beings of great power and influence. They could be called upon to influence a person's life or even judge those who err. However, a careless approach to the Orishas often ends in terror - you may incur the wrath, or another unwholesome result, should you approach an Orisha carelessly. And such carelessness is more often a result of ignorance rather than intention. The Yoruba culture and worship of the Orishas is not a DIY (do-it-yourself) project, and adequate knowledge, experience, and preparation are essential to proper worship of the Orishas.

Remembering that the Orishas operate via physical channels, especially through an oracle (graven image) and a priest, there's an easy way to worship the Orishas. It is simply by visiting the shrine of an Orisha, with an offering in hand and asking that the priest bless you and your offering. Offerings and prayers are important for worshipping the Orishas. Hence you cannot do without them.

Orishas According to Colors

To further explain how to worship the Orishas, they are split into two major categories: Orisha Funfun, the white-themed Orishas who are coolheaded and easy to approach (Orisha Obatala and Orisha Dudu), and the dark or red themed Orishas who are fierce and mostly hot-blooded.

Usually, errors or omissions in the process of worshipping white-themed Orishas are easily pardonable. But such pardon is not available with dark or red-themed Orishas. The difference is in the nature or color of each Orisha. This heavily determines what sacrifice or manner of worship is required.

Note, however, that no Orisha is to be toyed with. Acts of omission may be pardonable when summoning to a coolheaded Orisha, but that is a risk that should not be taken lightly. Just as a dark-themed Orishas can inflict terror or demand a blood sacrifice, a white-themed Orisha can also inflict terror or demand a blood sacrifice. It all boils down to this - blood is the ultimate seal of any sacrifice.

Simple Prayers

While worshipping the Orishas is not a do-it-yourself practice, there are simple and general ways to worship an Orisha. By engaging in simple prayers, you could call upon an Orisha without fear or error. Take, for instance, this prayer offered by Babalawo's when paying homage to Orisha Orunmila each morning:

Orunmila! Eleri Ipin

Ibikeji Olodumare

Ajeju Oogun,

Obiriti, Ap'ijo ikuda

Oluwa mi, Ato'baj'ayeg

Oro abikuj'igbo

Oluwa mi, Ajiki

Ogegg agb'ayegun,

Odudu ti ndu ori emere

Atunori tiko sunwon se,

Amoiku

Olowa Aiyere

Agiri ile-Ilogbon

Oluwa mi: amoitan

A ko mo O tan ko se

A ba mo O tan iba se ke

This prayer can be translated to:

Orunmila! The witness of fate

Second to Olodumare (The Supreme God)

You are much more effective than medicine

You are the great Orbit that averts the day of Death.

My Lord who is mighty to save,

The mysterious spirit who fought death.

Unto you are salutations first due in the morning

Great Equilibrium that controls the forces of the world

You are the One who works to help those with bad luck

Oh Repairer of ill-luck

He who knows you becomes Immortal

You are Lord, the undisposable King

Perfect in the house of Wisdom

Lord who is infinite in Knowledge.

Our failure to know you makes us futile.

Oh, if only we could know you in full,

Then all would be well with us.

Looking at this prayer, it can be deduced this is a matter of praising Orisha Orunmila each day. Trained devotees, priests who are known as Babalawo, engage in this prayer each morning in honor of Orunmila. Once this prayer is said, subsequent prayers (requests) can be tabled before the Orisha, requesting his aid.

Prayer Pattern

The way prayers generally work is that they first make you conscious of whatever entity you're praying to. Then you draw the virtue or unseen energy from such an entity to influence your life. Usually, the content of your prayers determines the influence noticed in your life.

So, to pray to an Orisha, understand the basic pattern of prayers. This pattern goes like this:

- Give praises to your chosen Orisha first.

- State your helplessness and need for the Orisha's help.

- Tell the Orisha about what you need help with - make your requests known.

- Round up your prayer with praises to the Orisha.

Once you have prayed, you may be tempted to doubt, but make sure you don't. Don't give room to thoughts like, "am I sure that worked?" Rather, be patient and keep your mind off the requests you've tabled. It is a general rule in prayers you first believe before you see any results. You first have to believe that an Orisha is potent enough to help you, then believe that your prayers are heard. Let go of doubts and watch for signs (no matter how little) that show that your prayers are being/have been answered.

Ashe

Faith or a strong belief in an Orisha and its supernatural ability is critical to receiving answers to your prayers. It is a foundational concept in many religions, and the Yoruba religion is no exception. As a rule, faith isn't just a matter of strong belief but also professing such belief. Faith in an Orisha must be shown not just via an action (sacrifice) but also via speech. People of faith are known for their daring manner of speaking, and it is a requirement if you want to see results. For example, a Babalawo, when summoning an irunmole - a lower-level spiritual entity or messenger to the Orishas, does not speak with fear but with authority. This is a mark of faith and confidence, and it is crucial when relating to the Orishas.

At times you may need to speak with humility, especially when it comes to petitions or calls for mercy. But at other times, a mark of your faith is your manner of speaking, which is where Ashe comes in.

By translation, Ashe means "so be it" and is a symbol of power and authority. It is the power that allows its user to speak things that relate to reality. An Alaase (user of Ashe) uses his speech to invoke supernatural forces that act based on his/her authority. Imagine a situation where you speak about healing, and a supernatural entity performs the act of healing you just spoke of.

According to the Yoruba religion, Ashe is within everyone. Some say that Olodumare, in blessing the human figures Obatala created, blessed them with Ashe. Like the Orishas who possess and perform wonders via Ashe, Olodumare blessed humankind with Ashe in a similar manner. It should be utilized to communicate with the Orishas and to control the course of one's life. By using Ashe alone, you can determine your destiny and also call upon the Orishas for help.

When praying to an Orisha, remember that you possess Ashe both as a means of authority and to communicate with the Orishas. Use it.

Ebo Riru (Sacrifice)

Virtually all religions agree that sacrifice is important in worship and prayers. Irrespective of the content, a sacrifice remains a sacrifice. Ebo riru loosely translates to sacrifice offered to the Orishas. It is a show of reverence and also guarantees answers to prayers. Depending on the size of your prayer request, your sacrifice could either be as little as a sacrificial meal or as great as a blood sacrifice.

Often, prayer or worship of an Orisha is incomplete without a sacrifice. In a certain respect, all that may be needed as a sacrifice could be kola nut or pouring of wine as a libation to the ground. The Yoruba religion strongly believes in sacrifice as a necessity for drawing on the powers of an Orisha. It helps with calling forth mercy and forgiveness where there is an error, and it also draws other virtues and blessings to the person who offers the sacrifice. It all boils down to this:

"Ebo riru lorisa ngbo."

- Afa'du Owanrin Meji

This translates to:

"Sacrifice is what the Orisha listens to."

Ebo riru cannot and should not be done carelessly. Depending on the situation that calls for a sacrifice, the consequences of error could be grave. A wrong or careless sacrifice is always rejected, and on certain occasions, attracts the wrath of the Orisha to whom the sacrifice was made. Hence, do not carry out a sacrifice all by yourself, especially without first answering these questions:

- What Orisha are you sacrificing to?

- What are the sacrificial meals and items peculiar to the Orisha?

- When and where are you to carry out the sacrifice?

- How do you carry out the sacrifice?

Usually, an experienced priest or devotee could help answer these questions and help you prepare your sacrifice in mind. While sacrifices are important, especially when the purpose of the sacrifice is great, you can still engage in simple prayers and keep your mind at rest.

Divination of Cowrie Shells

To utilize Ashe, knowledge and experience in divination becomes a must. You cannot efficiently utilize Ashe without having some level of experience in the divination of cowrie shells. This form of divination goes by many names but is particularly known in the Yoruba religion as Odu Ifa or Odu Owo Merindinlogun, which loosely translates to the Divination of Sixteen Cowrie Shells. In Santeria, it is known as Diloggun and practiced with strict principles.

The divination of cowrie shells is used to read fates. It allows a diviner access into supernatural secrets of the past, present, and future, and about a given situation. With these secrets, a diviner can ultimately influence fate by offering an alternative or positive change according to what he/she sees when divining.

.

Chapter 2: Olodumare the Almighty

Every religion and culture believes in a source. It is believed that the Earth was created and is governed by a singular entity existing outside space and time. In most cultures, this singular entity has subordinates created by him to ensure law and order - control over all creation. This is also true of the Yoruba religion that believes in the existence of one supreme entity and Lord over all - Olodumare. By translation, Olodumare means "the owner of the source of creation," which shows that Olodumare is just a manifestation of the Supreme God over all - Olodumare is not all there is to him.

According to the Yoruba culture, Olodumare – as the owner of the source of creation – total control over creation. While he may possess total control, he operates by delegation. Rather than being directly involved in the control of existence, he operates via his sons and daughters - Orishas who possess his virtues, traits, and powers. His sons and daughters are the ones who hold direct control and involvement in matters of creation, and they only operate because of his permission and tremendous power. They report to him.

Since Olodumare operates by delegation - he has no direct involvement in matters of existence. There is no shrine nor priest dedicated to him. According to the Yoruba religion, one can only access Olodumare via another Orisha. If you seek protection, call upon one of the Orishas, and he/she will respond based on your request. Olodumare considers mankind as the choicest of creation and, as such, tasks the Orishas with aiding the destiny of the sons and daughters of mankind. Hence, while you may pray to Orisha Sango for courage in the face of battle, know that Orisha Sango is only responding based on the guiding order received from Olodumare. None of the Orishas operate solely for their own purpose as they live and operate as emissaries of Olodumare to humanity.

Although there is no direct link to Olodumare, prayers can still be made to Olodumare. This happens especially when one either has no idea which Orisha to call upon or the Orishas are unresponsive to a person's call. Here, it is advised to pray directly to Olodumare, who often responds via an Orisha, i.e., he instructs an Orisha to respond. Consequent to the fact that he is the Lord over all other Orisha, none has any choice but to obey him. In all, Olodumare actively controls the realm outside space and time and lets his subordinate Orishas influence the course of creation.

Contrary to popular philosophies, Olodumare exists as the "uncreated creator." He has no beginning, and he has no end. While the laws of time and space may influence humans and their reasoning, it does not disturb Olodumare as he is the source of time and space. He can bend time, space, and natural laws to his will - this can be seen in the demonstration of power by his subordinate Orishas, e.g., the breathing of fire and summoning of lightning by Orisha Sango.

Olodumare vs. Olokun

Often it is said that Olokun is the rival of Olodumare and on an equal footing. While it seems true when you consider Olodumare as Olorun - the Ruler of the Skies, it's not 100% true. Agreed, Olorun rules the skies, while Olokun is the ruler or owner of the waters (both small and great), and it doesn't change the fact that Olokun at best is only on equal footing with a single manifestation of Olodumare as Olorun.

According to the tales of the creation of the universe, particularly the Earth, Olokun was an offspring of Olodumare's action. It so happened that when Olodumare created the universe, the energies present came together in obedience to Olodumare and took form. Amongst the created forms was Olokun, who was born out of the overall mass of hydrogen and oxygen. Olodumare's breath of life impacted every energy, and because of this, Olokun was created. In all, Olokun was the earliest Orisha ever created by Olodumare, and she had Orishas under her command, most being her daughters, who likewise controlled the water element.

Olokun should never be confused for Olodumare or even his manifestation as Olorun. Both rule over different realms and differ in authority. Olodumare rules over everything, including the heavens (skies) and the waters. Olokun strictly rules the waters beneath the heavens, albeit she can influence the heavens' waters in a similar manner. The Orishas submit to Olodumare as father and lord, while select Orishas submit to Olokun as mother and mistress. Olodumare has no equal in terms of power, but Olokun has a rival who rules over the waters in the skies.

In all of this, one thing is spelled out. The created can never be on equal footing with the creator. At best, the created can only express certain traits of the creator.

Olodumare - The Beginning of Creation

Like the Christian perspective of creation, the Yoruba religion believes there was nothing in the big black canvas of space. Olodumare was the only one existing, the only source of consciousness and reason. In his sojourn, he thought about making something meaningful out of the vast emptiness around him. That was the beginning of creation - his thoughts.

Olodumare, who possessed tremendous powers, breathed and gathered vast amounts of energies together - drawing them from all reaches of space. The gathering of these contrasting forms of energy resulted in an explosion of light first before taking on more tangible forms like stars, planets, solar systems, and the entire universe. But there's more.

Recall that before Obatala created dry ground and human figures for Olodumare to breathe upon, there was only the heavens above and the waters beneath. The existence of the heavens and the waters happened after Olodumare had caused the energies present to take form. Some merged to form the waters beneath the heavens.

Out of these waters came a form that can at best be described as a mermaid. It flicked its tail and caused mighty waves on the waters. Then a voice spoke from the form saying "emi olohun omi okun," which loosely translates to "I am the voice of the deep waters." This was the beginning of Olokun, who rules the waters beneath the heavens.

While Olokun dived deep into the waters after speaking, a shadowy figure was left on the surface of the water. It could be described as the residue of Olokun, which ascended above the deep waters. Her presence in the heavens helped form water clusters in the heavens, now known as the clouds. This "shadow" of Olokun is known by many as Yembo Olo'rure and rules over the waters in the heavens.

With the waters and the heavens created, Olodumare made great winds out of his breath to blow across the realm that was eventually the habitation of humankind. Although not giving life, these winds became crucial to the survival of all that had the breath of life in them. Thus, the air (wind) was given a greater purpose than just blowing across the Earth.

Names of Olodumare

To clear things up a little, here are the different names ascribed to Olodumare. Each name is a depiction of how he manifests himself to humanity. Humanity only came to ascribe these names to Olodumare, based on knowledge given to them by the Orishas. These names are often used in praise and also prayers directed at Olodumare himself. At times, the names are also ascribed to certain Orishas to signify the trait of Olodumare they carry.

Since introducing foreign religions such as Christianity and Islam to the African continent, lots of the names culturally ascribed to Olodumare have been syncretized as cultural names for God in these religions. As such, these names are sung, chanted, and repeatedly said in praise of God, who is the syncretized variant of Olodumare, the uncreated creator and source of all of creation.

1. Olorun

This is the manifestation of Olodumare that takes charge of the heavens. As ruler of the heavens and skies, he lords over the abode of the Orishas. The Orishas require his aid if they're to descend to the realm of humankind. Prayers are directed toward the heavens as it is the abode of the Orishas. Once they reach the heavens, only then can Olorun instruct the Orishas to respond to such prayers.

No mortal can get to the heavens in his/her mortal form, as it is strictly for the Orishas. It takes a great deal of sacrifice and a change of form before anyone can access the heavens.

2. Eledaa

This is the creative manifestation of Olodumare. He is the creator and giver of life and all other aspects of creation. The Yorubas believe that everything is tied to Olodumare via this aspect, and, as such, they constantly pray that the creator shields them from bad luck and curses.

3. Elemi

This is a manifestation of Olodumare known for preservation. He is the keeper of life, and everything owes its life to him.

In recent times, this name has been distorted to refer to a person with strong spiritual ties. Here, the person has difficulties in living normally due to being overwhelmed by the spiritual ties present in their life. This kind of person is said to live in between the spiritual and physical realm and often serves as a bridge between the Orishas and mortals.

4. Olu'ase

This name strictly refers to Olodumare as the source of all power and authority. From him, every other Ase is found, and without his Ase, none other can function. Being the source of all Ase, the title Olu'ase - the source and owner of authority, supersedes other variant titles bearing Ase, e.g., Apa'ase - the one who decrees with authority, which is often given to mortal men of high esteem such as kings and celebrated chiefs.

As the source of all authority, Olodumare is likewise prayed to when installing a new king in any Yoruba community. It is believed that the king possesses both divine and mortal authority, and prayers are made both as a show of his divine authority and a submission to the source of all authority, i.e., Olodumare.

5. Olulana

When there is no clear path to take in moments of confusion, Olodumare can be called upon using this name. Olulana loosely translates to "way maker." At times it may be translated to "way-finder," Olulana expounds on Olodumare's all-knowing ability in determining what step to take.

Olumoranokan Eda

It is often said that no one can know the intent of a person's heart, except that person. But the saying does not apply to Olodumare, who is the source of all. The name olumoranokan eda means he knows and is capable of revealing the intent of the heart. No one is outside his scope, and because of this, it is often advised that one thinks only good thoughts and banishes all forms of evil or negative thoughts. This refers to the attributed Olodumare because he is more of a judge of intent rather than action. He bestowed his virtue on Orisha Orunmila, which further taught mankind what is known as Iwa Pele (good character), which begins from within (the heart) and grows outward.

Anyone who wishes to be helped by Olodumare must first cleanse him/herself of evil thoughts or intent. To do this, one must first forgive anyone who has done them wrong and seek to make amends. Purity of heart is vital to be heard by Olodumare, who sees all and knows all hearts' intent. Neither Orisha nor any mere mortal can escape his gaze.

Qualities of Olodumare

It's important to discuss the specifics concerning the traits and qualities in Olodumare which make him stand out from the rest of the Orishas. These traits will help you understand more about Olodumare and influence your mode of approaching him in worship.

1. He is the First Creator

While it is easy to say that Olodumare is the Creator, it is important to state that he is not just a creator like Obatala was. Rather, he is the first creator who created every Orisha and even mortal man with the creative virtue to create even more things. Olodumare is both the first and supreme creator, to whom every other creator submits.

This is depicted in one of the Yoruba tales of creation, where it was said that the world was initially a marshy wasteland with ugly growth here and there. This was after the point when Olodumare created the universe, and the Earth was yet to be fully formed with solid ground, humans, and proper vegetation.

Olodumare and the Orishas lived in the heavens but frequented the marshy wasteland in-between the heavens and the deep waters - this was done via a divine chain. The purpose of visiting the wasteland was mostly for hunting and exercising their divine abilities.

On a certain day, Olodumare summoned Obatala and spoke to him about his desire to great solid ground. To do this, Olodumare gave Obatala a snail shell filled with sand, a hen, and a pigeon and sent him off. Acting upon Olodumare's instruction, Obatala, who doubled as Orisha-nla, descended into the wasteland via the divine chain. Once he'd reached a certain level, he poured the sand onto the marshy ground and lowered the hen to the ground. The hen promptly began scratching and scattering the sand, and by so doing, the sand was spread throughout the marshy surface. Obatala sent word back to Olodumare via the pigeon that he'd finished creating solid ground. Olodumare, in response, sent a chameleon he'd forged to go and inspect the work Obatala had carried out. The chameleon, upon inspection, reported that the ground was solid, but it was not dry enough. Olodumare waited for a while before sending the chameleon back to Obatala. As at this time, the ground had spread far and wide and was perfectly dry.

With the first phase done, Olodumare instructed Obatala to replenish the Earth with all necessary vegetation for life. Obatala, who had been given divine palm nuts, was to plant these which were, in turn, to sprout fees palm trees and replicate over and over until the Earth was full of vegetation. Equipped with the palm nuts which sprouted as Olodumare had decreed, Obatala was able to source palm wine, oil, and fronds with which he created the first shelter on Earth. Although Olodumare gave the instructions, Orunmila aided Obatala with his counsel on carrying out each instruction.

To populate the Earth, Olodumare told Obatala to create human figures out of clay and wait for him. Obatala did as he was told but could not give life to the forms. This was a unique trait of Olodumare as the life-giver (Elemi), and as such, only he could breathe life.

With each batch of humans he molded, Olodumare breathed on them, and they began living, but Obatala was curious and eventually envious of the life-giving power of Olodumare. His envy and curiosity grew to where he made more human figures and hid to watch Olodumare perform his life-giving act. Olodumare, who was all-knowing, knew what Obatala was up to. To handle the curiosity and envy of Obatala, Olodumare put Obatala into a deep sleep so he couldn't tell when Olodumare came around, breathed life into the new batch of human figures, nor even when he left the Earth after he had finished.

2. He is Omniscient

From the legend of creation above, another trait of Olodumare that could be seen is his omniscient nature. He sees everything and knows all things. While many focus on the outward, Olodumare sees both the intents of the heart and the actions of all - no matter how carefully hidden they may be. Because of this, Olodumare is known by another name, "Arinurode Olumoranokan," which means that he is "the one who sees the inside and outside, and knows the intentions of the heart."

3. He is Unmatched

Olodumare, being the first and supreme creator, is on a superior level to every other Orisha. Seeing as he is the source of all things, it is only natural for him to be unmatched. His powers and virtues are exemplary and serve as the basis for every other Orisha, who in turn teaches mankind. Even Olokun, who is, at times, confused as an equal rival of Olodumare, was born out of his acts of creation. She hardly compares to Olodumare's manifestation as Olorun - the Lord of the heavens, who can veto her authority when necessary.

Olodumare is beside himself in all things, the only one whose Ashe is uncontestable. There are no idols dedicated to Olodumare, and that is born out of reverence for his unmatched level. No painting or carving can describe Olodumare, as he is all in all.

4. He is the Immortal Source of Immortality

The Yoruba culture believes that Olodumare existed before the beginning and will continue existing beyond the end. Because he is known as Elemi - the giver and keeper of life, it is only to be expected that he is the source of life cannot die. And this goes to show he is immortal - this can be seen in a Yoruba oriki that says "a ki'igbo iku Olodumare" (we do not hear the death of Olodumare).

Beyond Olodumare's immortality, he is known to be the one who grants the souls of mortal's immortality. In a certain respect, some say that after a person dies, his/her soul returns to Olodumare, who reserves it until a moment of reincarnation (if he so pleases). In the same vein, the Orishas source their immortal and divine nature from him, and that is the only reason they have existed for so long - before man - and will keep on existing.

5. He is Omnipotent

The words "Olodumare l'oba a se kan" are parts of the praises given to Olodumare that mean "he is the king who works unto perfection." Due to his immense power and wisdom, Olodumare works intelligently and ensures that his works and instructions are carried out perfectly. This can also be seen in the tale of creation when he instructed Obatala and sent a chameleon twice to check the work's quality.

Anyone can direct prayers to Olodumare, pleading for him to help ensure that perfection is achieved in any project engaged in. He will respond through Orunmila, who possesses a greater portion of his wisdom, and that will prove helpful. The Yoruba adage summarizes his omnipotence and ability to bless works toward perfection - "a dun'se bi ohun ti Olodumare lowo si, a soro bi ohun ko lowo si" (whatever Olodumare approves is fun/easy to do, but where his approval is absent, such becomes difficult).

Chapter 3: White Orishas I: Obatala and Orunmila

Power comes in different forms. At times it could appear as fierce and destructive, and at other times power could seem as calm and neutral. Just because power seems dormant or inexpressive does not automatically mean there is no power. In the same vein, when power is seemingly expressed calmly, it should not be misunderstood as weakness. Power is dynamic – it can switch from momentary calm to full-on destruction. What matters isn't the potential of power to be either calm or destructive but the wielder of such power. It is often said that a weapon is only as powerful as its wielder, which is not far from the truth. Power likewise is only expressed based on the whims of its wielder.

With the Orishas, they are divided into two categories based on their expression of power. These categories are based on the colors red/black and white. Red/black colored Orishas are noted for their fierce and destructive expression of power, while the white-themed Orishas are known for their calm demeanor. It should be noted that the Yoruba culture does not categorize the Orishas based on the stereotype of good and evil. The colors do not identify an Orisha as evil, neither does it ultimately translate to an Orisha being inherently good. Rather, the colors are mostly based on each Orisha's preferences, and an Orisha determines the color he/she would like to be associated with.

Aside from being a matter of preference, the colors serve as a guide for ritual conduct among worshippers. The red/black themed Orishas often require blood sacrifice and a particular daring among their worshippers during ritual activities. But this is different for the white-themed Orishas, who rarely require blood sacrifice nor fierce display from their worshippers during ritual activities. A white-themed Orisha can require a blood sacrifice, while a red/black-themed Orisha could likewise not require a blood sacrifice – it mostly depends on the nature of what is being requested of the Orisha. In simpler cases, a simple ritual meal (ebo riru) is all that would be required. But the greater the request/need, the greater the sacrifice required.

Among the white Orishas is Obatala, who is first among them and known particularly as Orisha Funfun, Orunmila the source of divination, Aje the source of wealth, Osanyin the source of plant medicine, Yemoja the goddess of the waters, and Oshosi the source of divine focus. Each one of these Orisha is known for calm and ease of being called upon. They offer wisdom, protection, fertility, precision, guidance, and a ton of other positive virtues bound to make life easy and more fulfilling. Some are also affiliated with other light-based colors. For instance, Oshosi and Yemoja are associated with different shades of blue, Osanyin is associated with the greenness of plant life, and Orunmila is often represented with a similar color of green.

Obatala

Obatala is one of the elder gods of the Yoruba culture. He is one of the oldest Orishas in the Yoruba pantheons and is known as the creator of all human forms - who were breathed upon by Olodumare. In certain aspects, he is viewed as the father of all other subordinate Orishas.

Being the one who was tasked with creating the world (Earth), Obatala is honored as the creator of the world, while Olodumare remains the undisputed creator of the universe.

Obatala goes by many paths and is chiefly known for his affiliation with the color white. Orisha Funfun, as he is also fondly known, comes from his name, Oba (which means king), t'ala (which refers to an undyed fabric – a blank canvass on which other colors are cast to represent his varying paths). He is an embodiment of purity, both physically and spiritually, and is considered the light of all consciousness.

To Orisha worshippers, outside the shores of Southwestern Nigeria, Obatala is viewed as Jesus of Nazareth due to him being the savior and protector of mankind. This is aside from the fact that he is the creator of humankind – and the deformed whom he swore to protect.

Like other Orishas that marked or were reincarnated into humans, some say that Obatala was a one-time Oba (king) of Ife. His subjects duly revered him until the point when he lost the throne to Oduduwa (a helper turned rival in certain texts). The tale of his loss of the throne is to this day retold through traditional drama during the Itapa festival in Ile Ife.

While most Orishas have more male paths over female paths, Obatala is known for the existence of dual paths. His paths are equally spread between male and female essences, unlike the Orisha of wisdom – Orunmila, the custodians of Obatala's secrets are mostly female; there are more priestesses of Obatala than male priests.

Paths of Obatala

Just like Olodumare, Obatala expresses himself in different forms known as paths or avatars. These paths serve different purposes and, as such, can be petitioned based on specific needs.

1. Obatala Orisa Aye

This is a female path of Obatala that represents the mystical virtues of females.

2. Obatala Ondo

This is another female path of Obatala. This path is a virgin and lives within rocks at the edge of the sea.

3. Obatala Ayalua

This female path of Obatala is a warrior and destroyer. Obatala Ayalua is a variant and rival of her brother Ayalá.

4. Obatala Alabalashe

This path of Obatala speaks to his children in prophetic dreams. He stands for the past, present, and future.

5. Obatala Olufon

This path of Obatala cannot dwell in the darkness. As such, he needs light at all times – his shrine must always have a source of perpetual light.

6. Obatala Oloyu Okuni

This path of Obatala is the source and owner of the eyes of all humans.

7. Obatala Osha Orolu

This path is known as the king of Eg'wadó.

8. Obatala Okelu

This path is the king of Ekiti and Abeokuta; he lives in the highest of places.

9. Obatala Ana Suare

A male path of Obatala that accompanies Oba Moro. His children cannot throw anyone out of their home nor raise their hands in anger.

10. Obatala Oshalufon

This male path of Obatala gave mankind the ability to speak; he is of the king of Ifón.

11. Obatala Oguiniyan

This male path of Obatala allows no one to see his face.

12. Obatala Obalabi

This path of Obatala is the Originator of Oyó, and it is believed that he is deaf.

13. Obatala Elefuro

A female path of Obatala, the queen of the soil. She is also known as Imolé.

14. Obatala Oba Ayiká

This path of Obatala protects homes. People always ask this path for special protection of their homes and properties.

15. Obatala Oba Malu

This path of Obatala works in the hardest of times to help people overcome obstacles in their lives.

16. Obatala Efun Yobi

This path of Obatala protects his children and those of his enemies. He helps to alleviate pains in the legs and brings harmony to the home.

17. Obatala Alarmorere

This path of Obatala is represented by a saw and hammer of silver.

18. Obatala Orisha Yeye

This is another female path of Obatala and is seen as one of the eldest of the female paths of Obatala.

19. Obatala Ogbon

This path of Obatala walks with his brother Oggán. He oversees the journey of the spirits of Obatala's children when they pass on to heaven.

20. Obatala Aikalambo Male

This path of Obatala is the king of Iká, close to Ibadán. He was born in via Odu Ofun Sa.

21. Obatala Oshereilbo

This male path of Obatala walks with Sango at all times.

22. Obatala Airanike

This path is a warrior who walks with Oshalufón and is called Ajósupato in Arará.

23. Obatala Oyu Alueko

A male path of Obatala that is seemingly selfish, as he wants no other Orisha to have more children than he has.

24. Obatala Orisha Iwin

This path of Obatala is from Owó and is the protector of the palace of Obatala.

25. Obatala Oye Lade

This path of Obatala is a hunter and the king of Ekiti. He always walks with Oshosi, and in the Arará, they call him Bajelo.

26. Obatala Ekundire

A male path from the land of Iyesá accompanies Oduduwa.

27. Obatala Orisha Obrala

This is a young and virile male path of Obatala.

28. Obatala Bibi Nike

A male path of Obatala that constantly rides a horse.

29. Obatala Edegu

This path of Obatala is the king of the lands of Efushé.

30. Obatala Abgany

This path is a teacher of Iyebú. He is blind, lives in water, and is a preserver of life.

31. Obatalá Ayenolú

A male, also known as Yelú and Laguelu, in the city of Ibadán.

32. Obatala Agguidai

A male path of Obatala oversees the messages with Olofi. He has four stones and tools that are sealed, and they may not be touched by the sun, air, or dew.

33. Obatala Orisha Aye

This path of Obatala brought order to the world and gave Orunmila the secret of the Ase.

Oriki Obatala

There are different ways to approach Obatala. Simple prayers can be made to his name, and ritual meals can be placed before his shrine. But one of the easiest to do, which is most recommended for new worshippers and enthusiasts of the Yoruba religion, is to sing praises to the Orishas. These praises serve as a unique form of prayer and are known as 'Oriki.' Each Orisha has at least one oriki dedicated to him/her. Some are available to the general public and sung during festivals dedicated to the Orishas, but other oriki are sacred and only sung by experienced devotees and within closed circles.

Below is an oriki dedicated to Orisha Obatala:

Iba Obatala

Iba Oba igbo

Iba Oba n'le Ifon

O fi koko ala rumo

Orisa ni ma sin

Orisa ni ma sin

Obatala o su n'nu ala

Obatala o ji n'nu ala

Obatala o tinu ala dide

Adiniboiti ri, adupe

Ase, ase, asese o

This oriki translates to:

Praise to the chief of the white cloth

Praise to the chief of the sacred grove

Praise to the chief of the heavens

I salute the owner of the white cloth

It is the owner of white light that I serve

It is the owner of white light that I serve

Chief of the white cloth sleeps in white

Chief of the white cloth wakes up in white

Chief of the white cloth gets up in white

He who creates at will, I thank you.

So, let it be, so let it be, so let it be done.

Another fascinating piece of Oriki for Obatala:

Obatala, the strong king of Ejigbo

Seating at the trial, a tranquil judge.

The king whose every day becomes a feast,

The Owner of the brilliant white cloth.

Owner of the chain to the court of heaven.

Obatala stands behind the people who tell the truth,

The protector of the handicapped,

Oshagiyan, the warrior with a handsome beard.

He wakes up to create two hundred civilized customs.

It is he who holds the staff – Opasoro, the great king of Ifon.

Oshanla (mighty god), grant me a white cloth of my own

You who makes things white,

Tall as a granary, tall as a hill.

Ajaguna, deliver me.

You're the king that leans on a white iron staff.

General Notes on Obatala

- Orisha Obatala was the creator of the Earth and the human race. In certain texts, he was aided by the first man he created – Oduduwa, known as the father of the entire Yoruba race.

- Obatala is syncretized as Jesus Christ of Nazareth. At other times, he is associated with the Catholic saint Mother Mary.

The actual Yoruba culture greatly influences Santeria, Voodoo, and Hoodoo depictions of Obatala. There are only slight variations, and these are mostly seen in the names and oriki. For instance, while the Yoruba culture calls him

Obatala or Orisha Funfun, he is known as Oxala, Ochala, Orixala, Orichala, or Oshala in these religions.

- Obatala is worshipped to draw out virtues of peace, purity, and harmony in a person's life. This can be seen from his affiliation to white – a product of his name that talks about adding colors (meaning) to a white canvass (life).

- Obatala will never answer a person with evil intentions. Purity of the heart is important when calling upon Obatala.

- The ritual meals Obatala readily accepts are coconuts, white bread, milk, white rice, and water. These can either be accompanied by simple prayers or by praising him with his oriki.

Orunmila

Orunmila, known far and wide as Orunla or Agboniregun, is a major Orisha of the Yoruba tradition. He is the source of divine wisdom, knowledge, righteousness, and divination forms. His wisdom is so vast that it understands all there is to know about human nature, and he possesses the most effective purification methods. He is the one who founded divination and has his form of divination known as Ifa (the divine wisdom of Olodumare). Ifa divination is only available to a few people who dedicate their lives to learning and diving accurately with Ifa as an oracle. These devotees to Ifa divination are known as Babalawo (priests of Ifa) or Iyanifa (priestesses of Ifa).

According to Yoruba's accounts of creation, he was the Orisha who gave counsel to Obatala on what to do – how to create the dry ground and fashion man from clay. With the creation of man finally done, Orunmila joined his fellow Orishas to visit the earth. He dwelt among the Yoruba people as a priest – the founder of the Ifa divination system, teaching them the ways of Olodumare and how to commune with Olodumare. His powers of divination are always accurate and help to determine the destiny of a person. Popularly known as Igbakeji Olodumare, i.e., the second in command of the supreme God, Olodumare, he is greatly revered in the Yoruba culture, holding a special significance above the other Orishas. Orunmila's special place among the Orishas is mostly because Olodumare bestowed on him the virtue known as Ori (intuitive knowledge). This unique endowment gives him the power to intercede and influence the life and destiny of any person he chooses – and he can do this much more than his fellow Orishas.

Just like every other Orisha, Orunmila came to the Earth and taught mankind the ways of righteousness, wisdom, and divination – ways to call upon Olodumare. Realizing that his sojourn on Earth was not an eternal one, Orunmila knew there was a need to fill the vacuum that his absence would create He foresaw this and gave select people a greater portion of his wisdom, teachings, and skill in divination. These people were to serve as priests in his stead once he departed the surface of the Earth. They were to support his teachings and guide all who sought the wisdom of Olodumare about their lives and difficulties.

The selected people were given the title Awo Ifa which loosely translates to the priest of Ifa. Ifa priests were mostly adult males who had gone through sacred training. The gender limitations were broken over time as certain women showed potential in Ifa divination. Just like the males who underwent training, females chosen by Orunmila were permitted to undergo sacred training before their full initiation. Rather than being called Awo, the females had the unique title of Iyanifa, which loosely translates to mother of Ifa divination.

Duality is a principle in Ifa divination – this refers to the fact that both the male and female are critical to existence and balance - the male cannot exist without the female essence. The female cannot exist without the male essence. Hence, just as there are males initiated into Ifa divination, females were required to be initiated too. Interest and personally being chosen by the oracle play a key role in being initiated.

Odu Ifa

The Yoruba culture greatly honors Orunmila as the greatest priest to have ever walked the face of the Earth. Aside from being an Orisha who existed before the Earth's creation, he also served as a priest of Olodumare during his stay on the Earth. It was during his moments on Earth that he created the divination system known as Ifa.

Odu Ifa referred to a divine collection of stories and prayers possessed by Orunmila and passed down from generation to generation through his chosen priests and priestesses. There are 16 major books under Odu Ifa, and each book has 16 subdivisions of secrets accessible to only the priests and priestesses of Ifa. These 256 Odu Ifa are said to contain all probable situations, decisions and actions, and consequences in anyone's life. With these, the priests and priestesses of Ifa knew and required wisdom to give counsel and guidance to anyone who sought their help. Irrespective of sacrifices that may be required to remedy whatever situation one may find him or herself in, the works of righteousness, also known as Iwa Pele, often saved someone from total damnation.

Although most of the prayers of Ifa divination are sacred and only accessible to the priests and priestesses of Ifa, here is a more generic prayer dedicated to Ifa. It is directed toward the human Ori (spiritual head), which greatly determines a person's destiny.

> *Ori, mo juba (I honor you and give you thanks),*
>
> *It is you who is with me through all the events of life.*
>
> *Ori's l'ori mi (I have a good Ori - head)*
>
> *Ori ire (good Ori) that links me to Olorun*
>
> *Ori ire, that is Olorun's essence in me.*

Ori ire that is open to receive the blessings that Olorun sends to me

Ori're l'ori mi (I have a good Ori - head),

Ori ire that is open to the wisdom of Ifa

Ori ire that is open to the guidance of Orunmila.

Ori ire that receives assistance from the Orishas - gods.

Ori ire that welcomes and embraces Egungun - the spirits of the dead.

Ori ire that welcomes assistance from Egungun.

Ori're l'ori mi (I have a good Ori - head)

Ori, I beseech you to keep my doors open

Ori, I ask that you always bring me blessings

Ori, I beseech you to always support me in tough times,

Ori, I beseech you to always rejoice in good times with me.

Ori, I embrace you, and I ask that you always embrace me.

Ashe, Ashe, Ashe o (a variant of Amen - so let it be).

Oriki Orunmila

Orunmila Eleri Ipin

Ibikeji Olodumare.

Akeju Oogun,

Obiriti, apijo Iku da,

Oluwa mi, atoibajaye

Oro abiku jigbo.

Oluwa mi, ajiki.

Ogege agbaiye gun.

Odudu ti n du ori emere,

A tun ori ti ko sunwon se,

Amo iku,

Olowa aiyere,

Agiri ile ilogbon.

Oluwa mi amoimotan,

A ko mo o tan ko se.

Aba mo o tan iba se ke.

Mojuba akogda,

Mojuba aseda

Akoda ti n ko gbogbo aiye ni Ifa

Aseda ti n ko gbogbo agba n'imoran

The translation is:

Orunmila, the witness of fate,

The second in command to Olodumare (Supreme God).

You are far more effective than medicine.

You are the one who averts the day of death.

My Lord, the almighty to save.

The mysterious spirit that fought death,

Unto you salutations are due first in the morning.

You are the equilibrium that adjusts the forces of the world

You are the one whose exertion it is to reconstruct the creatures of bad luck.

You are the repairer of ill luck.

He who knows you becomes immortal.

Lord of the King that cannot be deposed.

Perfect in the house of wisdom.

You are the lord who is infinite in knowledge.

By not knowing you in full, we – your servants are futile.

If only we could know you in full,

All would be well with us.

I praise the first created

I praise the creator

The first created who teaches the whole world the divination of Ifa

The creator who teaches the elders wisdom.

General Notes on Orunmila

- Wisdom and righteousness are the hallmarks of Orunmila. His devotees are expected to walk in the righteousness of heart and actions.

- Orunmila is a diviner that can foretell the destiny of anyone. Where there is uncertainty or evil ahead, Orunmila can be called upon for wisdom on how to avoid such evil. He can rewrite destiny, but only in agreement with the person concerned. Such a person needs to be ready to work according to instructions. Otherwise, there will be no change in destiny.

- Variations in the worship of Orunmila in Santeria, Voodoo, and Hoodoo religions are mostly based on the blend between actual Yoruba and the predominant language in places such as Cuba, Brazil, and Latin America, where these religions are predominant. As such, Orunmila is mostly known as Orula in Santeria.

- Orunmila is worshipped so that a person can walk in wisdom and depth of perception. This way, a person isn't just sensitive to happenings, as a person who calls on Orunmila is further endowed with the wisdom on how to live, act or react, to forestall problems.

- A true devotee of Orunmila must be righteous, i.e., clear of bad intentions and actions. Forgiveness and slowness to anger or picking offense are crucial to a devotee.

- While perfection is seemingly impossible, devotees of Orunmila are encouraged to grow, taking each step at a time to live righteously.

Chapter 4: White Orishas II: The Water Gods

The Yoruba culture has a unique reverence for women. This stems from the duality belief that the Earth comprises both male and female energy. Both energies exist in harmony to ensure balance. It is believed that the creation of the world was incomplete without the input of female energy. Out of the universe's creation, Olokun was formed and became a crucial part of the creation of thriving life forms on the Earth. Obatala could not carry out Olodumare's instruction without first receiving permission from Olokun to create the solid ground on the surface of the waters she controlled.

It is believed that women possess a dual nature of calm and destruction – depending on whichever is entreated. A woman's touch can either bring about calm and prosperity, or it can cause total downfall. In virtually all cases, it is the lives of men that are greatly influenced by the virtues that flow from women. This shows that the male energy, which is most fierce, requires female energy's calming virtues. Since the female energy is mostly calming and dynamic, most of the female Orishas are affiliated to the color white and are predominantly controllers of the water element. Osun, for instance, was known for her beauty and calming influence over

Orisha Sango, and her virtues are implored to help women become more desirable to their husbands. Female Orishas are predominantly white Orishas, and that goes to depict not just their calming virtue but also their beauty, prosperity, and creativity.

Recalling what was said about the two types of Orishas, female Orishas are also capable of great terror. Orisha Oya is a typical example – as a matter of fact, she is mostly associated with the color red, which symbolizes her ferocity. She is the only female Orisha actively engaged in her husband's military might – she reinforced Orisha Sango's powers and assisted him actively in military campaigns. Her thunderstorms always made it easy for Sango to summon lightning upon enemies, and as such, victory was guaranteed in most cases. Orisha Oya shows that female Orishas are not all about calm and beauty but are also a fierce power that must be reckoned with.

Olokun

Just as every Orisha is sourced from Olodumare, the first creator, every female Orisha – particularly those who control the water element are born out of Olokun. Olokun is the overall patron goddess of the deep waters and the Orishas who rule over the waters. She is the source of all the waters on Earth and is praised for her ability to minister good health, prosperity, and fertility to those who call on her. It is believed that none of the children of Olokun can suffer barrenness, as she is believed to be the source of fertility. Based on the belief of duality, Olokun is seen as both female and male, but she predominantly operates as a female Orisha.

According to the tale of creation, Olokun had always governed the waters after she was born out of Olodumare. There was no cause for alarm nor disagreement as she was in harmony with Olorun. When Obatala carried out the creation of solid ground, it turned out to be a breach of her authority. She hadn't yet given her consent, and he'd already begun his descent – in a certain context, as he had already poured the sand out of the snail shell, and the solid ground had already formed.

Angered by the encroachment on her territory, Olokun, who resided in the deepest parts of the waters, rose violently to the surface and began submerging everything in water – the first humans that existed were at risk of being drowned, and they desperately cried to Obatala for help. Realizing his error and being unable to pacify Olokun, Obatala sought counsel from Orunmila, who instructed him to fashion the longest chain he could ever create and use it to subdue Olokun. After this, Obatala sought the aid of Ogun, the god of iron, to help with the creation of the chain. This was quickly done to ensure all was not lost to Olokun's rage.

With the long chain, Obatala battled with Olokun taking her back to her territory in the deepest parts of the oceans where he chained her down, thus reducing the effects of her temper on the waters. One thing was certain, Obatala was acting on Olodumare's instructions, and although Olokun's temper was seemingly justified, she could not go against Olodumare's command. Because of this, her reacting in anger to Obatala executing Olodumare's instruction was seen as rebellion. Eventually, Olorun had Olokun pacified. An agreement was reached, and the waters were restrained from crossing into the land. Hence, no matter how far the water moved, it was made to recede to its source in honor of the agreement.

In all the stories about Olokun, her outbursts often caused great manifestations in water bodies around the area. Some say that during her reincarnation as the senior wife of Oduduwa, she was engaged in a heated rivalry with one of her subordinate wives, and that led to the birth of the Atlantic Ocean far away.

Oriki Olokun

Olokun aje ti aye oba omi

Omi nla to kari aye

Osele gbe senibu omi ti koni momo

Gbogbo eni ti waje

E je ka kori si ile Olokun

Sanle aje

Iya eni to l'aje

Iya eni to l'aje

Ogbugbu ni so oni so boji

Alagbalu gbu omi

Alagbalu gbu omi

Eni ajiki

Eni ajike

Ai ri di Olokun

Ao mo bere re

Aje pe gbogbo omi

E fi ori fun Olokun gbogbo odo

E fo ori fun Olokun oba omi

The translation is:

The owner of the waters and prosperity – the Queen of the realm of waters

The great waters that cover the Earth

A wonderful ocean that has no end

Whoever seeks wealth, let them go to the house of Olokun who has abundant wealth

Mother of uncountable wealth

Mother of uncountable wealth

Waters without end

Waters without end

The one we greet when we wake

The one whom we cherish

No one knows the source of Olokun

No one knows her beginning

Prosperity calls unto all the waters

Let the waters bow to Olokun

Crown Olokun as the Queen of the waters.

General Notes on Olokun

- Olokun is the source of all water-based Orishas. She is the mother of Yemoja, Oya, Osun, Aje, and every other minor Orisha affiliated with the water element.

- Olokun operates via duality. She is predominantly female and manifests with the male energy at certain points.

- Santeria, Candomble, and other Yoruba-oriented religions in the diaspora recognize Olokun as a powerful Orisha, but just like Olodumare, she is not directly worshipped.

- Olokun is the source of wealth - a virtue she bestowed predominantly on her daughter Orisha Aje who is worshipped directly.

Yemoja

Yemoja is an Orisha that controls waters and is also known as the second in command of Olokun - she is the eldest daughter of Olokun. According to Santeria, she has been syncretized as the Catholic saint, the Virgin Mary. This is also replicated in the Afro-Cuban areas where she is known as "Our Lady of Regla." Virtually all the names borne by Yemoja point toward her affiliation with motherhood and the Virgin Mary. Names like Yemaya, Madre del Agua, La Sirene, among others, demonstrate this. They point to her being a protective mother who is sourced from the waters.

As an Orisha, Yemoja is protective of her children – all of humanity - and she shares in their joys and sorrows. When the Yoruba Empire fell, and many were taken out to sea to be sold as slaves, some say that her devotees cried out to Yemoja, the mother of the waters, to console them of their loss and help them find strength and courage during turbulent and strange waters. Yemoja responded by bringing calm to the sea waves, keeping the hearts and minds of the people strong until they were able to reach land and continue the Yoruba tradition.

Besides being a mother to all, Yemoja has a soft spot for her female children (women) and offers them the cure to infertility. An infertile woman only needed to offer sacrifice to Yemoja, and in return, Yemoja would offer one of her eggs to the woman to encourage fertility. Yemoja takes charge of all things that pertain to women – especially the areas of childbirth, nurturing, love, and healing.

As a mother of the waters, Yemoja is mostly calm and associated with blue and white colors. She is responsible for the calm waves on the rivers and seas, but she can also rise in anger, and that can cause a tempest. Here, devotees promptly offer sacrifices to appease her and restrain the tempest. Where the tempest persists, prayers are made to ensure that life is not lost to the tempest.

Due to the vastness of the sea and the fact that it is the resting place of uncountable riches, it is believed that Yemoja owns the riches hidden deep in the waters. Because of this, her symbol includes cowries sewn into clothes of white or blue colors. She is often prayed to by fishermen to bless their voyage and ensure they rake in bountiful fish harvests.

Like her mother, Olokun, Yemoja is often illustrated as a mermaid. But generally, she is seen as a beautiful Nubian woman walking on the surface of the waters. The moon is also a symbol of Yemoja and can be seen in most illustrations about her.

Paths of Yemoja

34. Yemoja Yembo (Yemu)

This path of Yemoja is the mother of all Orishas and is the source of the crown of Yemoja. She is often said to be Oduduwa in female form.

35. Yemoja Ibu

This path of Yemoja is married to Orisha Aganyu, and they often meet on the riverbank.

36. Yemoja Ibu Oleyo

This path of Yemoja was born in Odun Ogunda – Iroso. She is a lover of fish and hens and is always dressed in light blue.

37. Yemoja Ibu Olowo

This path of Yemoja was born in the Odu Odi-Iroso. Yemoja Ibu Olowo is the owner of all the riches trapped in the depths of the waters.

38. Yemoja Ibu Okoto

This path of Yemoja was born in the Odu Merunla – Iroso. She is said to live in conch shells.

39. Yemoja Ibu Asesu

This path of Yemoja is the patroness Orisha of the ducks, swans, and geese. She is the revered messenger of Olokun and requires patience when being called upon.

40. Yemoja Akere

This path of Yemoja lives in the deepest parts of the ocean and is born of the Odu Odi-Ojuani.

41. Yemoja Oro

This path of Yemoja works with egungun (masquerade spirit) and operates mysteriously.

42. Yemoja Achaba

Born out of the Odu Osa Mesan, this path of Yemoja talks about her royalty and is often represented as an anchor. Some say that she is the one who finds shelter in the anchors.

43. Yemoja Okute or Okunte

This path of Yemoja was born of Odu Ogunda Meji and served as the wife of Ogun. She is a warrior - patroness of the Amazons and is a hard worker.

44. Yemoja Mayelewo

This path of Yemoja is the favorite daughter of Olodumare. She was born in Odu Irosun Ofun and lives at the bottom of the ocean. Her chief virtue is that of stability.

45. Yemoja Ibuagana

On this path, Yemoja is the wife of Orisa Oko and is born of the Odu Iroso-Metala. While she is said to be beautiful, she has seven lumps on her abdomen and has one leg thinner than the other.

46. Yemoja Atarawa

This path of Yemoja is said to be the owner of treasures found both in the ocean and on land.

47. Yemoja Ibubunle

This path of Yemoja is born of Odu Eye'nle Meli. She lives atop reef rocks and has symbols such as a hook, sword, seashells, and paddles, among others.

48. Yemoja Ibu Akinomi

This path of Yemoja dwells in the water's waves and is born of Odu Eye'nle Odi.

49. Yemoja Ibuconla

This path of Yemoja is born of Odu Odi-ejila. She builds ships and is often seen as a poet or muse for poets.

50. Yemoja Ibuina

This path of Yemoja is a warrior and doesn't shy away from disputes or wars. She is born of Odu Osa-ogunda. Her preferred meat is that of carp and goats.

51. Yemoja Ogunayibo

This path of Yemoja is born of the Odu Marunla-Ogunda and is known for her large breasts. She is a warrior who works with Orisha Ogun and is the patroness Orisha of older women.

52. Yemoja Ogunosomi

This path of Yemoja works with Ogun and Sango. She is a warrior who lives on the surface of the waters and also climbs mountains. She is born of the Odu Iroso-obara.

53. Yemoja Ibunodo

This path of Yemoja dwells in rivers and is symbolized with a silver chain.

54. Yemoja Yemase

This path of Yemoja has a mighty crown on which seven ritual cowries, machetes, and axes are hung. These are further supported with a boat and an arrow from Orisha Oshosi.

55. Yemoja Ibualaro

This path of Yemoja can be described as the Orisha of life and death.

Oriki Yemoja

Agbe ni igbe're ki Yemoja ibikeji odo

Aluko ni igbe're ki'losa, ibikeji odo

Ogbo odidere I igbe're k'oniwo

Omo at'orun gbe 'gba aje ka'ri w'aiye

Olugbe rere ko, Olugbe rere ko, Olugbe rere ko,

Gbe rere ko ni olugberere

Ase!

Translation:

It is the bird that takes good fortune to the Spirit of the Mother of the Fish – the assistant to the goddess of the Sea (Olokun)

It is the bird Aluko that takes good fortune to the Spirit of the Lagoon – the Assistant to the goddess of the Sea (Olokun)

It is the parrot who takes good fortune to the Chief of Iwo

Children are the ones who bring good fortune from Heaven down to the Earth

The Great One who gives good things, The Great One who gives good things, The Great One who gives good things,

Give me good things from the Great One who gives good things.

So, let it be.

General Notes on Yemoja

- Yemoja is one of the seven most worshipped Orishas in Brazil

- She is perceived as the guardian Orisha of fishermen and sailors during shipwrecks. Tons of shipwreck survivors testify to being pulled to safety by an unknown force and also having visions of mermaids and sweet voices while struggling to survive in the water. This has been attributed to Yemoja as the mother of "fish children" – mermaids who instruct her children to rescue shipwreck victims.

- Yemoja is seen as "Our Lady of Seafaring" in Salvador – a Catholic symbol for safety on water voyages.

- Yemoja accepts offerings like flowers, porcelain dishes, mirrors, jewelry, and other feminine items.

- Festivals attributed to Yemoja are held on these dates, February 2, September 7, December 8, and 31.

Osun

Osun, the most beautiful and favorite queen of Sango, is an Orisha that works hand in hand with Orunmila – the Orisha of wisdom and Ifa divination. Osun, also known as Ochun or Oxum in Latin America, is one of the daughters of Olokun and is also a water-based Orisha in the Yoruba pantheon. She is the goddess of the Osun River that flows between Osun and Ekiti in Southwestern Nigeria. She aids fertility, love, beauty, and the overall appeal of women. She is also active in divination, just like Orunmila.

According to Yoruba mythology, Osun was the female Orisha whose energy ensured that all that was created was beautiful. Some say that when Olodumare decided to create the world, the male Orishas began the creative process without the female Orishas' influence. The world lacked form and beauty – a special power solely attributed to the female Orishas. Osun, who was to lead the female Orishas in influencing the course of creation, was ignored, and, because of this, she went to her partner Sango for help. Sango, who was known and feared among all other Orishas, forced the other Orishas to listen to Osun and accord her the same respect they accorded him. It was only then that they listened to Osun, and the world began to take shape beautifully. As it is said, a woman's touch is what makes things beautiful.

Paths of Osun

56. Osun Ibu Kole

This path of Osun works with a vulture. She serves as a watcher over homes and eats whatever sacrifice is brought by her vulture.

57. Osun Ololoridi

This path of Osun is a fighter and a proponent of revolution. She welcomes change borne out of struggles.

58. Osun Ibu Akuaro

This path of Osun likes eating with her sister Yemoja and is known to her children by a secret name.

59. Osun Ibu Ana

This path of Osun is the owner of drums.

60. Osun Anani

This path of Osun is argumentative. To invoke this path is to prepare to defend one's case before help is released.

61. Osun Ibu Yumu

This path of Osun is famous for her beauty. She has no suitor due to her being deaf. It is uncertain if her deafness is figurative or literal.

62. Osun Ibu Odonki

This path of Osun lives where the stream is born. She is the essence of the mud of the river and the owner of the streams.

63. Osun Ibu Ogale

This path of Osun is an old fighter that hates being disturbed.

64. Osun Ibu Akuanda

This path of Osun was born in the Odu Ikafun and is known for freeing Sango after Oya imprisoned him.

65. Osun Ibu Adesa

This path of Osun is a preserver of royalty. Her name means that she is the one who has her crown well secured. She owns a faithful peacock.

66. Osun Ibu Alade

This path of Osun works hand in hand with Eshu.

67. Osun Akuase Odo

In this path, Osun was said to be stillborn and works with spirits - especially those of the dead.

68. Osun Ibu Bumi

This path of Osun has a personal Eshu that she works with.

69. Osun Ibu Eleke Oni

This path of Osun is blessed with a good character aside from her beauty.

70. Osun Ibu Itumu

This path of Osun is a patroness Orisha of the Amazons. She is a warrior who rides an ostrich into battle.

71. Osun Ita Timibu

The path of Osun is a communal leader and only manifests at night.

72. Osun Ibu Aremu Kondiamo

This path of Osun is born of the mountains. She lives on an Ifa divination table.

73. Osun Ibu Semi

This path of Osun lives in areas around the rivers.

74. Osun Ibu Fonda

This path of Osun is a warrior who died at war.

75. Osun Ibu Odoko

Osun works with Orisha Oko in this path; she is known as a farmer in this case.

76. Osun Ibu Awuayemi

This path of Osun speaks via Odu Oyekun Meli – she is blind and walks with five bronze canes and a horse.

77. Osun Ibu Idere Lekun

This path of Osun dwells in caves and always rejoices anytime the waves hit the ocean reefs. She wears a mask to hide her deformed face. This is the only path where Osun is seemingly ugly.

78. Osun Ibu Inare

On this path, Osun lives on wealth and is the daughter of Ibu Ana.

79. Osun Ibu Agandara

This path of Osun was born in Odun Ikadi and is always found sitting in a chair with a lock.

80. Osun Oroyobi

On this path, Osun is gifted with precious sands by Olokun. She prefers salmon as her favorite ritual meal.

Oriki Osun

Iba Osun sekese,

Latojuku awede we mo

Iba Osun Olodi,

Latojuku awede we mo.

Iba Osun ibu kole,

Latojuku awede we mo.

Yeye kari,

Yeye 'jo,

Yeye opo,

O san rere o.

Mbe mbe ma.

Yeye, mbe mbe l'oro.

Ase.

The translation is:

Praise to the Spirit of Mystery,

The Spirit who cleanses me inside out.

Praise to the Spirit of the River,

The Spirit who cleanses me inside out.

Praise to the Spirit of Seduction,

The Spirit who cleanses me inside out.

Mother of the mirror,

Mother of dance,

Mother of abundance,

We sing your praises.

Remain (exist), exist always Mother,

Exist always in our tradition.

So, let it be.

General Notes on Osun

- Osun worship is done on the bank of rivers – especially the Osun river.

- Osun only accepts ritual meals placed in white or yellow dishes. Where a sacrifice is not accepted, it remains in the same spot. But when accepted, the water's tide will pull the sacrifice into the water.

- Osun provides wealth and beauty, which is shown in her symbols such as gold and copper. She is often depicted as a beautiful woman and only offers her virtues for wealth and beauty to women.

- Osun is syncretized with the Catholic saint known as "Our Lady of Charity," which is a reminder of her being a symbol of love and beauty. Just like her sister Yemoja, she is also depicted with the moon.

- In Santeria, Osun is known as Ozun. Other varying names are accorded to her in Hoodoo, Voodoo, and Candomble (where she is known as Nkisi Ndandalunda).

Chapter 5: Other White Orishas

The Orishas are known for their immense power, but how they express their powers determines what category of Orisha they fall into. For those who are associated with the color white, these are predominantly calm and easy to be entreated. But be wary that you do not incur their wrath due to carelessness or ignorance. Every Orisha is a force to be reckoned with – never to be toyed with.

As it is said, there is more than a countable amount of Orishas existing. Some are only worshipped and recognized in households, while others are known on the far-off shores of Africa. Despite how much an Orisha is known, one thing is certain – such an Orisha is an embodiment of power and influence over devotees' lives. The Orishas can also touch Non-devotees, but that depends on the circumstances – it could be an answer to the prayer of a devotee or an unexplainable stroke of divine intervention. Consequently, the White Orishas are more important than the majors listed in the preceding chapters. There are many more whose knowledge is hidden in cults and households, but in all – what matters is that a White Orisha can be asked for help without a necessary threat to life, and this is best done aided by a devotee. Simple prayers and offerings just in reverence of an Orisha are welcomed, but you need to give the right offering, say the right prayer and chant the right praises if you want to be accepted. When in doubt of what offerings to give, do not make an offering – you shouldn't give an offering at all and then risk wrath due to error and ignorance. One thing is certain. You can never go wrong when giving praises. A simple greeting, such as "Orisha Aje mo juba" – Goddess of wealth, I greet you, is a good start. You can always chant rich praise or give a worthy offering after you've done the needful research and preparation under the guidance of an experienced devotee.

With all that said, let's get down to other White Orishas worthy of mention:

Oba

Orisha Oba is one of the daughters of Yemoja (conversely an offspring of Olokun) and a major Orisha in the Yoruba pantheon. Unlike most Orishas, with different names in Santeria and other Yoruba-oriented religions, Oba is known far and wide only by her name. Still, she is syncretized as the Catholic Saint Catherine of Siena.

Although she is not as widely known as her sister Orisha - Osun and co-wife - Oya, she is a water goddess in her respect. She is the patroness of River Oba that flows from Igbon in the Yoruba region of Nigeria. According to Yoruba legend, she served as the senior wife of Sango but was to a great extent the least loved. Oba is forever at enmity to Osun, who tricked her into cutting off her ear and feeding it to Sango – to have their husband love her more. While there are variations in Oba's tale in Santeria regions, her rivalry with Osun is the most prominent. Oba's hatred for Osun was born out of the trick played on her where she asked Osun for help in getting Sango to love her more. Osun, who was the most loved, rather than helping her co-wife (which is seemingly understandable as she wanted no rival to hold Sango's heart), resorted to trickery. She informed Oba that Sango was in love with her due to her sacrifice - she cut off her ears and fed them to Sango. Although Oba did not believe this initially, she was convinced when Osun told her there was nothing to worry about since the ears always grew back fast.

Yielding to the outrageous counsel by Osun, Oba cut off her ears to feed her husband. However, rather than endearing her to Sango, this singular act made him furious to where he exiled her from the palace. Some say that Oba exiled herself out of shame in other variations to the story - she did not want her husband to see her without ears, neither did she wish to give her rival a chance to mock her continually.

From the legend, one thing is clear, and that is the fact that desperation was the undoing of Oba. But that, to a great extent, is understandable. She was the eldest wife who had to bear the excesses of a virile husband - Sango. His subsequent marriage to Oya and Osun was hurtful to her. With the new wives' presence, she gradually receded into the background where she hardly commanded the attention of Sango, and with this change, her desperation was fueled.

Consequent to her being tricked by Osun and being the least loved among the wives of Sango, she became revered as the patroness Orisha of exploited hearts. Oba is said to console hearts that have been broken or are lovesick.

Like her fellow Orisha and wife, Osun, Oba controls bodies of water and is a daughter of the Yemoja. Her rivalry is seen to this day at the confluence of the River Oba and River Osun – the consistently turbulent crashing of water at the confluence of both great rivers is seen as both Orishas fighting eternally.

While devotees sing the praises of Oba, such praises are not commonly known. In the same vein, prayers and unique details concerning sacrifices and days of worship are mostly known by devotees – a pointer to the fact that Oba is mostly shrouded by the shadow of her co-wives' shadow Orishas, Oya, and Osun.

Aje

Aje is one of the daughters of Olokun – the Mother of the Waters and Seas, and because of this, she has a strong command of the natural element of water, just like her sister Yemoja. However, in Yoruba mythology, Aje is strictly known as the principal Orisha of Wealth. In Santeria, Orisha Aje is known as Aye, who at other times manifests as Aye Shaluga, and she works with Osun in blessing her children with wealth.

All matters of business, money, and wealth are ascribed to Orisha Aje, who is often called Aje Olokun, i.e., Aje, the daughter of Olokun. Market women, traders, and even hunters who sell bush meat pray to her before selling their items. A common Yoruba greeting among traders says, "aje a wa o," and it is a short prayer to Orisha Aje to bless their businesses - it simply means "there will be sales." This greeting that doubles as a prayer to Orisha Aje, also draws the virtues of wealth or opportunities for wealth toward whoever says the prayer. It is both a communal and personal means of growing wealth.

Aside from being the Orisha of wealth, Aje goes by a principle of working to earn. A lazy person cannot pray to Aje, and only those who work can pray to Aje to bless their work and make them wealthy. It is often said there is no food for a lazy man. This means that only those who are diligent in business can discern when Aje creates an opportunity to provide wealth. This is an added confirmation that hard work will surely pay off. Aje can only bless the work of your hands, not hands folded in laziness.

To offer sacrifices to Aje, you must include one or more of the following: bananas, ekuru - a special type of corn cake, honey, or beans. Aje likes sweet meals and will bless based on the sacrifice offered.

Nana Buluku

Nana Buluku is an Orisha that appears as an older woman. She goes by many names in Santeria, Voodoo, Candomble, and other Yoruba cultural religions. She can either be called Nana Buruku, Nanan-Bouclou, and, in certain contexts, Nana Buluku. Among the Catholic Saints, she is identified as Saint Anne and Our Lady of Mount Carmel (the mother of the Virgin Mary). She is a white-themed Orisha who also operates fiercely. She can be likened to Orisha Oya, who is a fierce Orisha of the water element. However, Nana Buluku controls the earth. In her possession are her traditional ileke, casha, and ja which are unique to her. She accepts offerings like tobacco, garlic, rum, cypress, coconuts, coffee, tomatoes, and shrimp, particularly on her feast day, the 7th of July. It is advised that you do not ask for anything from Nana Buluku without being an initiate. At best, non-devotees can only honor her with their offerings or seek the assistance of an experienced devotee to help with their request. Nana Buluku detests offerings placed in iron plates or bowls. This is due to her enmity with Orisha Ogun, who offended her greatly. Because of this, she commanded her children never to come to her with any item of Ogun the Orisha of iron.

As an Orisha, Nana Buluku is worshipped majorly in Ghana rather than in the Yoruba regions of Nigeria. This stems from her being the supreme deity of the Fon people of Dahomey, who share ties with the Yoruba race. She is the patroness Orisha of women - a fierce protector who will not allow her children to be abused. As a fierce protector, Nana Buluku offers her aid in healing, pregnancy, justice, and rape. She even aids women in terminating unwanted pregnancies - especially those caused by rape. Nana Buluku is often termed stubborn because she never changes her mind.

Nana Buluku lives in the swamps and prefers being alone. At best, only her children or grandchildren may stay with her. According to legend, Ogun tried invading her swamp but lost his battle due to his metal rusting. Due to his futile invasion attempt, Ogun irritated her by being abusive to his wife - Nana Buluku detests domestic abuse of both women and children. Because of this, she responds angrily, even willing to eliminate an unrepentant abuser.

Nana Buluku is the mother of the divine twins who maintain balance over all creation, Lisa the sun god, and Marwu, the moon god. In a certain context, she is the mother of Babaluwaye, who is the patron Orisha of healing. Due to her affiliation with the earth and nature, Nana Buluku detests any actions against the earth. Poaching, wanton felling of trees, and pollution of all forms can incur the wrath of Nana Buluku.

Nana Buluku possesses immense wisdom and healing virtues, which she often grants to her devoted children. Some say that for one to become a daughter of Nana Buluku, she would have to give up the ability of childbirth while helping others with fertility issues.

Osanyin

Osanyin is an Orisha of the Yoruba pantheon who goes by Osain, Ossaim, or Osoin in Yoruba-centric religions such as Santeria and Candomble Voodoo, and the likes. He is syncretized as the Catholic Saint Joseph and is known for healing and herbal medicine. All forms of herbal medicine are sourced from Osanyin, who has divine knowledge about all plants in existence. He is an Orisha of divination in his own right and works – at times–with Orunmila.

Herbalists under Osanyin are known for their in-depth knowledge about plants and their medicinal attributes. It is often said that while science takes long to find a cure, herbalists under Osanyin only need to look at the plants and make the cure. This is a pointer to the fact that Osanyin isn't just a healer of spiritual illnesses but also an active healer of natural illnesses. At times illnesses are self-inflicted, but that makes little difference to Osanyin, who heals without discrimination.

For herbalists to heal, they resort to drawing on the powers of Osanyin via his iron staff (it is said to be the storehouse of Osanyin's powers). The staff, which is known as Opa Osanyin, and at other times called Opa Erinle, is used during the process of divination and is often placed on the floor beside the sick. It is designed with a crown on it upon which sit 16 small birds looking inward and a larger bird in the center looking outward. According to Yoruba belief, the staff symbolizes the dominion of good over evil and supernatural forces. Factually speaking, the smaller birds represent witches capable of transforming into birds to aid the healing process being carried out by Osanyin, who is the large bird in the middle. It should be noted that the birds on the staff possess various meanings. While some perceive the bigger bird as Orunmila, others perceive the smaller birds as messengers from Ogun symbolized as the bigger bird, who aid the healing process of Osanyin.

A proverb is common to herbalists under Osanyin, and it speaks of the duality of the powers of leaves. Some say that "the leaf which can cure you, can also kill you" Hence, care must be taken when using plants for medicine.

Oshosi

Oshosi is the Orisha of the forests. He controls all life and wealth in the forests and is the one who permits hunting. In Candomble, he is known as Oxóssi, while in Santeria, he is known as Ochosi and is syncretized as the Catholic Saint Hubert. He is depicted as a man with a bow and arrow and with a stag standing beside him - these are likewise the symbols of Oshosi. In other contexts, Oshosi is syncretized with Saint Sebastian in Rio de Janeiro and syncretized as Saint George in Bahia.

It should be noted that the Orishas were syncretized with Catholic Saints by the Yoruba people, who were sold as slaves. It was a means to cover up their religious practices from slave masters who detested such practices. Thus, wherever the enslaved Yoruba people were moved to, they syncretized the Orishas based on Saints with similar attributes such as Orisha. Hence, Oshosi, for instance, is syncretized with three different but similar Saints - his worship is made on the celebrated days of such Saints viz-a-viz 20th January for Saint Sebastian, 6th June for Saint Hubert, and 23rd April for Saint George.

Oshosi is known as the source of food or meat and is known for his swiftness and wisdom in hunting. He accepts mostly animal sacrifices such as goat, guinea fowl, and pig. He also accepts cooked maize, yams, and black beans, among other vegetables.

Oshosi is greatly worshipped in Brazil due to the presence of the Amazon and is often seen as a lone Orisha who comes and goes into forests in a bid to consult plants. Eshu, Osun, Ogun, and Oshosi are the Orishas known as Warriors in Santeria and Candomble. Some say that Oshosi was the only Orisha to ever declare war on Ogun due to a disagreement. Normally, Ogun starts wars due to him being the Orisha of war, but in this case, he was challenged by Oshosi. Although the battle was fierce and long, neither was defeated and because of this, a truce was formed. The truce eventually grew to be a long-standing friendship due to the respect they had for each other's fearsome powers.

Ori

Each person is believed to have their own deity, called Ori, who controls destiny. To entreat Ori into granting good fortune in a person's life, cowrie shells are used to design a sculpted oracle for the Ori.

Ori, who is otherwise known as Ori Inu (the Head Within), is a major factor in what happens in a person's life. Fate is decided in the shrine or dwelling place of Ori. Ori is the foundation upon which human personality dwells. While some are born with certain personalities, Ori can be influenced to be changed or influenced for the better. A person with bad manners is bound to get into trouble. But Ori can be appealed to for a change of such a personality.

However, this can only work alongside the person's willingness to shed such personality traits.

Ori is further worshipped as a means of spiritual balance and guidance in each person's life. While consulting Ifa is good when a person wants clarity and knowledge about his/her destiny, Ori is personally available to all. Before consulting Ifa, Ori is readily within reach of consultation. Ideally, Ori is consulted first before Ifaas; at times, what Ifa reveals will require a person to appease Ori first before further actions are carried out.

The potency of Ori varies in each person. Some closely commune with their Ori, while some are ignorant of Ori's existence. Hence there is confusion and no clear direction for life. Regardless, each person can develop a cordial relationship with his/her own Ori by engaging in prayers and greetings to Ori. Think of it like blessing your day each morning and night. This way, whatever is being said to Ori - the prayers or greetings ultimately draw in virtues to a person's life. Whether such virtues are positive or negative is determined by the individual.

Chapter 6: Dark Orishas I: The Trickster and the Warrior

The dark ones are often seen as harbingers of destruction and evil. But that is not entirely true. Agreed, they are expressive in a temper and exude an aura of intimidation; the dark Orishas, or those predominantly associated with the colors red and black, are not all shades of evil. Orishas such as Ogun, Sango, Oya, Esu, and Aganju, among others, are known as dark Orishas due to their ferocity. But it doesn't mean that they are evil. At worst, Esu is known as the Orisha of mischief – and his mischief is often directed toward erring persons. Orisha Ogun doesn't just start wars – there is always a reason for every war. The dark Orishas are known summarily for their terror, which is a fundamental reason for them being worshipped and celebrated greatly.

Esu

The best description that can be given to Esu La'olu Ogirioko is none other than a trickster. As an Orisha, he can be likened to Loki of the Norse pantheon due to his mischievous nature. Pronounced Eshu and known as Exu in Latin America, he is the Orisha of trickery, mischief, crossroads, death, and chaos. He is also the Messenger (Elegba) to all other Orisha. Some say that Esu manifests in 256 paths when acting as Elegba the Messenger to all other Orisha – according to Ifa divination. However, Ocha divination says that Esu only manifests in 101 forms. He could either manifest as Esu Aye, who worked hand in hand with Olokun, or he could work with Sango and Oya devotees as Esu Bi – a fierce path that appeared either as an old man or young boy. Esu Bi is known for protecting and playing with children – particularly twins. At other times, and most often, Esu works with Osun, where he takes the path as Esu Laroye – a diminutive and talkative oracle.

Out of all the 256 paths of Esu, the path known as Esu Odara is the father of all other paths of Esu. Legend has it that the paths of Esu were created during his fight with Iku (the spirit of death). After a prolonged battle, Iku struck a seemingly fatal blow by slicing Esu into two. However, out of the halves sprang two new Esu. Surprised but unmoved, Iku kept cutting down Esu, and Esu kept on increasing, birthing new replicas until the battlefield was overfilled. Iku, who tired of the battle, turned and fled, leaving Esu to deal with his clones.

Aside from his fight with Iku, Esu, when he served as Elegba to other Orishas, must manifest in forms unique to each Orisha he is working with. It follows, he created new forms of himself that would take on different appearances fitting to each Orisha he worked with. Thus, it is often said that Esu is as uncountable as the Orishas of the Yoruba religion. Some say that Esu is the divide between the Orishas and evil forces or demons known as Ajogun. While the Orishas counter the actions of the Ajogun in the lives of mankind, Esu stays in between both parties as a mediator. He is both a messenger to the Orishas and the leader of the Ajogun. The Ajogun serve as his emissaries of mischief and judgment. Out of 201 Ajogun, Esu has eight chiefs. They are Iku, the spirit of death who he fought with before birthing his new paths; Arun, who is the spirit of all sickness; Egba, who is the spiritual source of paralysis; Epe, who is the spirit of all curses; Ewon the spirit of imprisonment;

Oran who is a troublesome spirit; Ofo who is the spirit of misfortune and grave loss; and Ese who is the spirit of error and all other forms of the problem.

Depending on the path Esu decides to take, he must never be toyed with as the slightest error from anyone will make him unleash havoc through his unending supply of mischief. In a certain context, Esu is said to carry a bag where he stores his mischief. At times the bag is depicted as big, and at other times it's very small, but whichever size it is, the bag is said to be limitless, and hence Esu can never run out of tricks.

When engaging Esu, one requires patience and wisdom to get the best of Esu, who likes playing on intelligence. Esu helps make decisions, striking a balance between good or sensible decisions and bad or foolish ones. As the Orisha of crossroads, he offers help when confusion sets in. Good decisions can be made through Esu, and these will cause success, blessings, and ease, but where bad decisions are reached, Esu doesn't hesitate to reel out the consequences trapped in such terrible decisions. This ultimately points to the fact that although the Orishas influence the course of a man's life, free will to make decisions and take actions is solely controlled by man. You are made or marred by the decisions and actions you take. It is only wise to seek the wisdom of the Orishas before carrying out your plans.

Paths of Esu

81. Esu Laroye

This path is one of the youngest of Esu. He is behind every door and loves joking around, playing pranks, and is overly mischievous. He is a good friend and messenger of Osun.

82. Esu Lagu'na

This path of Esu is known for his strength and is the patron Orisha of Egungun (masquerades which are the spirits of the dead).

83. Esu Bi

This path of Esu is always seen at crossroads. He breeds discord, doubts, and misfortune on erring persons. His lessons are always taught via painful and, at times, deadly mischief. Where the required lesson is not learned, he doesn't hesitate in dishing out more punishment. Here, Esu can either be your best friend or your worst enemy – you need to be wise when dealing with him.

84. Esu Anaki

This path of Esu is seen as a female. Esu Anaki is an enforcer of law and order among the numerous paths of Esu. She instructs each path on how to commune with humans and also the other Orishas.

85. Esu Aina/Bara Aina

This path of Esu is a messenger too and works hand in hand with Orisha Sango. He is the one who opens the way for Sango when he goes to battle.

86. Esu Arerebioko

This path of Esu is the path that works with Ogun. Esu Arerebioko accompanies Ogun whenever he goes on adventures or hunts in the forest.

87. Esu Aye

This path of Esu walked the seashores. This Esu knows all that we want. Aye also means the world – hence he knows the secret places of riches and mundane pleasures common to humankind.

88. Esu Elegbara

This path of Esu is a carrier of good fortune and blessings to his followers.

89. Esu Alaketu

This path of Esu sits on the outskirts of the town of Ketu in Africa. He is a wise man that brings fortune to the town.

90. Esu Afra

This path of Esu is from Arara, the land of Dahomey. Esu Afra is a close friend of Asojano. He is received when one receives Asojano.

91. Esu Ana

This path of Esu is the owner and path to the sacred drums. He opens the path for communication between the sacred drums and the Orishas.

92. Esu Ashikuelu

This path of Esu lives at the entrance of the marketplace. He is a great negotiator and is used to settle issues relating to money.

93. Esu Bara Layiki

This path of Esu is carefree and loves dancing or partying.

94. Esu Dako

This path of Esu resides in the forest. He knows the herbs and how to hunt.

95. Esu Alboni

This path of Esu resides high in the mountains.

96. Esu Ayeru

This path of Esu is the messenger of Ifa.

97. Esu Aroyeyi

This path of Esu guards the entrance to Olofi's castle.

98. Esu Ode/Ode Mata

This path of Esu walks alongside Ochosi in the hunt.

99. Esu Owo

This path of Esu guards all the riches of the world.

100. Esu Beleke

This path of Esu loves to play as a child. He loves to dance and brings good fortune to those who deserve it.

101. Esu Eluufe

This path of Esu is aged and wise. He doesn't like to be disrespected under any circumstances. He grants wisdom to those who seek and are worthy.

Oriki Esu

Esu,

Esu odara,

Esu la'olu ogirioko

Okunrin ori ita

A jo langa lau

Arin lanja lalu

Ode ibi ija de mole

Ija ni otaru ba d'ele ife

To fi de omo won

Oro Esu, to akoni

Ao fi ida re lale

Esu ma se mi o,

Esu ma se mi o,

Esu ma se mi o.

Omo elomiran ni ko lo se.

Pa ado asubi da

Na ado asure si wa

Ase o!

This translates to:

Divine Messenger,

Divine Messenger of Transformation,

Divine Messenger speak with power.

Man of the crossroads, dance to the drum,

Tickle the toe of the drum.

Move beyond strife,

Strife is contrary to the Spirits of the Invisible Realm.

Unite the unsteady feet of weaning children

The Word of the Divine Messenger is always respected

We shall use your sword to touch the Earth.

Divine Messenger, do not confuse or hurt me,

Divine Messenger, do not confuse or hurt me

Divine Messenger, do not confuse or hurt me.

Confuse or hurt the child of another (instead).

Turn my suffering around

Give me the blessings of the calabash.

So, let it be.

General Notes on Esu

- Esu is the Orisha of crossroads and can help with indecision

- Esu, being a mischievous Orisha, does not like dull people. He plays a lot on intelligence and will often reward intelligence greatly.

- Esu is both a messenger and a chief. He serves other Orishas but stands as the chief of the Ajogun.

- Esu is the first to receive sacrifice before any other Orisha in a festival or ceremony – he is the messenger and must be petitioned before carrying a sacrifice to a particular Orisha.

- Esu is known as Eleggua in Santeria. He is also known as Elewa – the handsome one, and Elegbara, among other names in Yoruba-centric religions in the diaspora.

- Due to his mischievous nature, he is known as Exu in Candomble, a variant name for the devil.

- Esu is a witness to the past and the future – he needs no form of divination to recall the past or foretell the future. The past is a culmination of decisions and actions, just as the future is determined by decisions and actions – and he governs these decisions and actions.

- Olodumare blessed Esu with the divine keys to every sacred door, so he is deemed the first among other Orishas.

Ogun

Ogun Lakaaye, also known as Ogum in Latin America, is the Yoruba god of iron and war. Incarnated as a powerful warrior who became the first Ooni (king) of Ife after the exit of Oduduwa, he is greatly respected among the Yoruba people and the Haitians, Brazilians, Cubans, and in certain parts of West Africa. He is the patron god of blacksmiths, metal workers, craftsmen, and warriors who wield metal weapons.

According to Yoruba mythology, before Ogun became reincarnated into a man, he was the Orisha known for creating pathways. With his sword, cutlass, or ax in hand, Ogun cleared the path for other Orishas to find their way to Earth – particularly Ile Ife where Obatala dwelt. With his faithful companion – a dog, Ogun is often praised as the first Orisha to have come to the Earth, as every other Orisha had to wait for him to pave a path for them to follow.

Regarding his incarnation into a mortal man, Ogun was the first Ooni of Ife, a powerful one who commanded respect from subjects and enemies alike. When a person disrespected him, Ogun had the person executed swiftly by beheading.

Some say that Ogun Lakaaye was one of the most active and responsive Orishas even after departing from Earth. Being the god of war, rather than dying from a self-inflicted wound, he descended into the ground with a vow to respond quickly to anyone who called upon him. Acting on his promise, anytime there was a threat of war or raiders came to disturb Ire Ekiti's peace where he dwelt, the people only needed to run to his grove and call his name for help. Once he was called upon, Ogun would sprout out of the ground in a fierce whirlwind with his sword in hand and rush into the community where he would butcher anyone who looked threatening. It was advised that every indigene of Ire Ekiti stay indoors lest they got cut down by Ogun during his vengeful attacks on invaders.

Ogun came to the aid of Ire Ekiti's people for years until his power was eventually abused. Some say that Ogun stopped surfacing when a group of drunks summoned him from his grove, claiming that there was war in the land. As usual, Ogun sprang into action and killed everyone in sight. As it turned out, he realized he had killed innocent but drunken people instead of invaders.

Angered by their folly, Ogun vowed never to resurface again since they had toyed with him. But mercifully, he was willing to intervene through the wisdom and might he bestowed on Yoruba warriors.

Ogun Worship

Ogun Lakaaye being the patron Orisha of blacksmiths, hunters, and warriors, is represented by an iron (sword), a dog, and palm fronds. He is often revered as the Orisha of truth because anyone who swore by Ogun (kissing a piece of iron and calling on Ogun) would be forced to tell the truth or risk being struck down by him.

Being the god of iron, Ogun worshippers utilize all sorts of iron items during festivals and celebrations of Ogun. Items such as knives, local Dane guns (for hunters), iron chains, swords, blacksmith equipment, wrenches are displayed during the Ogun festival.

Although Ogun had a dog as his companion, sacrifices made to Ogun are incomplete without the beheading of a dog held apart by its head and hind legs. Ogun being the patron Orisha to hunters, mostly calls for sacrifices of bush meat. However, he will receive other forms of sacrifice such as kola nuts, Emu Ogidi (palm wine), palm oil, cockerels, salt (due to its iron content), snails, yam, alligator pepper, and water.

Paths of Ogun

102. Ogún Onile

The owner of the land. He is called Ogun Onile due to his nature as an explorer. He is praised for discovering new territories, animals, and even water bodies. This title means he was the first to come to an uncultivated place and settle in and was the first to work the land.

103. Ogún Alagbo or Alagbede

This path of Ogun is a blacksmith and serves as the patron Orisha of all blacksmiths. He is a hard worker who tirelessly works day and night. Due to his nature, he is anti-social or rude as all his time and attention are focused on his work rather than holding conversations.

104. Ogún Meji/ Ogún Bi

This path of Ogun has two faces. One is the representation of a good and hardworking parent who is peace-loving. The second face, however, is extremely violent, destructive, and bloodthirsty.

105. Ogún Arere

This path of Ogun is strictly a butcher.

106. Ogún Shibiriki

The creator of all things metal and is also called the murderer. He is always jealous of Sango and fights over the love of Yemoja. He is fierce, brave, and of great courage. Fighting is second nature to him.

107. Ogún-Kobukobu

This path of Ogun is known as the foreman. He is often seen with a whip in his hand.

108. Ogún Aguanile

This path of Ogun is a conqueror. He is the one who lords over mountains and newfound lands.

109. Ogún Adaiba

This path of Ogun is a warrior who shows love via his machete.

110. Ogún Jobi

This path of Ogun is a warrior who constantly lurks in bushes and ambushes his prey and enemies. He is violent and doesn't hesitate to react with destruction.

111. Ogún Adeola

The warrior who became king. He wears his crown with honor and reigns with wisdom, overseeing his people's safety and welfare.

112. Ogún Já

This path of Ogun is known for violence and is a fierce warrior. He is said to savor a blood bath in place of bathing in water. He feeds on dogs and causes a lot of arguments and violence if left without attention.

113. Ogún Oloka

A title associated with Ogun being the owner of the lands, and he is known as a farmer. He works the land and owns the fields and what is grown. He is praised for his good harvests and is also known as Olorukó, Olokuló.

114. Ogún Aroyo (toye)

This path of Ogun is known for being violent and impulsive. He is hot-tempered and highly irrational. He serves as the palace's best guard, as he reacts swiftly to what he perceives as a threat.

115. Ogún Onira

This path of Ogun is associated with rain, mud, and the murky waters of the river. This name was given to him because, in this path, he was king of the town of Ira.

116. Ogún Onire

This path of Ogun is known as a conqueror, warrior, and general of armies. He was once the king of the city, Ire.

117. Ogún Oké

This path of Ogun is known as the owner of the mountains and also goes by the names Afanamule and Ogún Ogumbí.

118. Ogún Aladú

This path of Ogun declared war on Yemoja at different times.

119. Ogún Valanya or Ogún Valenyé

This path of Ogun is known as the tiller of the ground.

120. Ogún Niko

This path of Ogun serves as an assassin.

121. Ogún Olode

This path of Ogun is the head of the hunters.

122. Ogún Soroka

This path is known as 'the highest speaking' path

123. Ogún Wari

This is another path of Ogun characterized by violence and destruction.

Oriki Ogun

When venerating Ogun, this Oriki (praise chant) is usually rendered:

Ogun Lakaaye o!

Ogun alara ni n gb'aja

Ogun onire a gb'agbo

Ogun Ikole a gb'agbin

Ogun gbengbena oje igi ni'imu

Ogun ila a gb'esun isu

Ogun akirin a gb'awo agbo

Ogun elemono, eran ahun ni je

Ogun o, makinde ti n dogun leyin odi

Bi o ba gba Tapa a gb'Aboki

A gba Ukuuku a gba Kemberi.

This translates to:

Ogun Lakaaye o!

Ogun manifests in seven paths

Ogun of the town of Ilara is the one who accepts a dog for atonement

Ogun of the town of Ire will accept a ram for atonement

Ogun of the town of Ikole will accept a snail for atonement

Ogun of the town of Gbenagena drinks tree sap for atonement

Ogun of the town of Ila accepts yam seedlings for atonement

Ogun of the town of Akirin accepts the fleece of rams for atonement

Ogun of the town of Elemono eats tortoise for atonement

Ogun o, the brave that wages war with aliens/foreigners

He will destroy either Nupe or Hausa

He destroys alien/foreign people and will destroy Kanuri too.

General Notes on Ogun

- Ogun is the Orisha of iron and all forms of war. Great wars and minor disputes are sparked by him and always interest him.

- While Ogun is known for warfare, he is also known for his wisdom and a prosperous ruler in different contexts.

- Ogun is the patron of discovering and conquering new lands.

He predominantly requires meat sacrifice, especially dog meat. But he welcomes other meals such as kola nuts, Emu Ogidi (palm wine), salt, and the likes. Blood is a predominant requirement of Ogun.

Chapter 7: Dark Orishas II: Shango and Oya

Among the hot-tempered, dark Orishas lies the power couple Orisha Sango and his fierce wife, Orisha Oya. They're predominantly warriors whose powers complement each other, thus guaranteeing them certain victory in battle – for the most part.

Sango

Sango is a fiery Orisha of the Yoruba pantheon known for his predominant color, red. In a certain respect, white or black is added to a red cloth in honor of him. Sango (pronounced Shango), who is known in Latin America as Xango or Chango, is the Orisha of thunder, lightning, and fire and evokes fear in the hearts of any who dare to defy his might. As an Orisha, he is the embodiment of male power, virility, and "merciless" justice.

According to Yoruba history, Sango was initially an Orisha before he was reincarnated into Arabambi, the son of Oranmiyan. His maternal grandfather sensed that Arabambi had been marked by the Orisha of thunder and lightning, and hence he gave him the appendage Sango in recognition of his true identity as the reincarnation of Orisha Sango. Arabambi Sango grew to be a fierce young man known for taming and playing with leopard cubs.

As a strong young man, Sango danced only to the beat of his own Bata drum (he had a dedicated Bata drummer who followed him wherever he went – to festivals, battlegrounds, fighting challenges, etc.). However, due to his principle of never dancing to the sound of other drums, except his own Bata, he drew jealousy from fellow dancers and spectators who mocked him for dancing only to the Bata drum. Arabambi, who was hot-tempered – a personality trait drawn from the Orisha within him, sought for the power to breathe fire. His quest to breathe fire proved successful as his mother's people from Tapa aided him.

Over time, Arabambi Sango grew stronger and was crowned as the third Alaafin (king) of Oyo. He took over the throne of Oyo from his elder brother Ajaka who was deemed a weakling. According to Yoruba history, Oyo suffered from raids carried out by warriors of Owu, an inferior Yoruba kingdom. All this happened during the reign of Ajaka, and it got so bad that the king himself was captured by the raiders – a humiliating experience for Yoruba royalty as they would rather die than be taken captive. It took the might of Sango to rescue Ajaka and restore Oyo as a military powerhouse in the Yoruba kingdom.

Sango's reign was one of might and terror as he engaged in countless wars, which he constantly won due to his fearsome nature and command of the natural elements thunder, lightning, and fire. His command of the elements was obtained from a charm known as edun ara, which his mother's people had bestowed on him. Sango was known for his sacred double-edged ax and had three wives Oya, Oba, and Osun, who became powerful Orishas of the Yoruba pantheon. Oya, the third and most powerful wife, is greatly respected by Yoruba warriors for her active participation in her husband's military campaign. Being the goddess of mighty winds and storms, her powers complemented him greatly, making it easy for him to summon thunder and lightning.

Although Sango brought about great prosperity and expansion to the Yoruba kingdom – no one would dare attack Oyo while he was the Alaafin -his fierce temper became his undoing – he ended up striking his palace with lightning. This act caused the wildfire to spread beyond the palace. An uprising of the people ensued against him, and they demanded he stepped down as Alaafin. In response, Sango left the city along with his chiefs and members of his royal cult known as Baba Mogba.

Some say that Sango hung himself on an Ayan tree in the region of Koso in some accounts. But this has over time being declared false by Sango's devotees. According to them, a usurping general Gbonka ambushed Sango and his party while he was leaving Oyo. However, Sango, who was grieved and unwilling to fight, turned and disappeared into thin air. He later appeared in the sky with fury and summoned lightning upon Gbonka, his ambush party, and the peddlers of rumors he – Sango had hung himself. Hence, he is revered as Olukoso, which means the king did not hang.

Sango is greatly worshipped in Yorubaland. His followers possessed a peculiar protection in that they could easily summon the wrath of Sango on anyone who wronged them, believing him to mete out due punishment. Seen as one of the most powerful Orisha in the Yoruba pantheon, Sango worshippers are governed by a unique code. Just like the fearsome Orisha, his followers braid their hair and attach cowries to it. While they may offer foods of worship such as bitter kola, amala, and gbegiri (mashed beans) or soup, Sango followers are forbidden from eating cowpea as that would incur the wrath of Ogun, the god of iron, and Sango's patron Orisha.

Paths of Sango

124. Sango Obadimeyi

This path of Sango signifies the relationship between Sangó and Aganju, his twin brother. Sangó and Aganju must be attended to equally.

125. Sango Obakoso

The title that Aganju was given after ascending the throne of Oyó, which meant the return of Sangó.

126. Sango Bum

In this path, Sango is seen as the son of Obatala and Yemoja.

127. Sango Dibeyi

This path of Sangó depicts the relationship between him and the children he bore with Osún; these children are known as Ibeyi.

128. Sango Alafi

This path of Sango is linked to royalty, government, legislation, law, justice, and superiority. Sangó Alafi is well respected for his authority and a great sense of justice.

129. Sango Arira

In this path, Sangó is the owner of the rains. He is present in times of rain, puts an end to the drought, and brings peace.

130. Sango Olose

In this path, Sango is the owner of the double-edged ax and holder of power. Sangó Olosé is a great warrior and strong character, and his words were never doubted.

131. Sango Kamukan

Sangó Kamúkan works with egun and has dominion over life and death.

132. Sango Obara

Sango is poor and raggedly dressed in this path, yet his word is the law, and he never lies. The house touched by the beam of Sangó Obara will be deserted and cursed.

133. Sango Jakuta

Sangó Jakuta is a path of Sangó, which means 'the stone thrower.'

134. Sango Ko So

Sangó Ko Só is a path of Sangó, which means "he did not hang himself." This relates to the events that occurred after the death of Sangó, the fourth Alaafín of Oyó.

135. Sango Bara Lube

This path of Sangó was the master of divination before Orunmila.

136. Sango Olufina Kake

This path of Sangó is the owner of the ceiba tree. Some say that he is the creator who sets fire to the roads.

137. Sango Obalube

Sangó Obalúbe is a path of Sangó, which means "The king who attacks with the knife." It was in this path that Sangó met his wife, Oyá.

138. Sango Obaluekun

Sangó Obaluekun is the appellation of Sangó, which means "the king who hunts leopards."

Oriki Sango

This is one of the best Oriki sung in honor of Sango and is best enjoyed with the beat of Bata:

Sango Olukoso!

Akata yeri

Arabambi Oko Oya

Alaafin ekun bu, a sa

Oloju Orogbo

Elereke obi

Eleyinju ogun'na

Olukoso lalu

Ina l'oju, ina l'enu

E'egun tin yona l'enu

Orisa ti n bologbo leru

San'giri, la'giri

Ola'giri Kankan figba edun bo.

A ri igba ota, sete

O fi alapa segunota

Ajisaye gbege oko Oya

Oloju Orogbo, Sango Olukosoooooo!

The translation for this is:

Sango the king of Koso,

The strong and mighty man.

Arabambi, husband of Oya.

The great and terrible ruler (of the palace) with a tiger.

The one with the eyes of bitter kola,

Whose cheeks are like kola nut.

Whose eyeballs are like coals of fire.

With fire in his eyes, and fire in his mouth.

The great masquerade that spits fire.

The god that is feared by all.

Sango the strong and mighty one.

With his might he reclaimed Edun.

He is unmoved by the sight of a thousand enemies.

He smites his enemies with his double-edged axe.

The one who awakens to impact the lives of all who call on him, the husband of Oya

The one whose eyes are like bitter kola, Sango - king of Koso.

General Notes on Sango

- Sango's sacred numbers are 4 and 6.

- Devotees always worship Sango on the fifth day of the week. This day is christened Ojo Jakuta, where Jakuta is a nickname for Sango.

- Sango is known in Santeria as Chango and is the most feared Orisha. Devotees in Palo call Sango Siete Rayos, while Haitians call him Ogou Chango.

- According to Candomble, Orisha Sango was the patron Orisha of slaves in the New World Plantations and was responsible for stirring them up into aggressive resistance.

- Bata gained popularity worldwide due to Sango and his devotees who dance solely to Bata.

- Sango leaves his mark on items by having them struck by lightning. When this happens, the item is moved to a shrine of Sango.

- Where an immovable item, e.g., a rock, is struck by lightning, Sango devotees convert the area around the item into a sacred site for worship.

Oya

Oya is the fearsome Orisha of wind, lightning, and violent storms. In a certain context, she is known as the goddess of death and rebirth. Oya, who is often called Iya Mesan (due to her giving birth to 9 stillborn children), was the beloved wife of Sango who participated in her husband's wars and ensured his victories in battle with her powers. She is the Orisha of the River Niger that splits the Yoruba territory from the Hausa/Fulani territory of Northern Nigeria.

Being a fierce Orisha in her own rights, Oya, just like her husband, is a fierce warrior who wields a sword and is revered among Yoruba warriors. She is associated with the color red and has control over the dead.

According to Yoruba history, Oya loved her husband Sango greatly but was the cause of his downfall. In the Yoruba folklore, Oya hid Sango's sacred stones (the ones imbued with edun ara), so he would not act rashly toward her. She knew he needed them, and hiding them gave her some sort of respect from Sango. Her plan worked, and he carried her along on his military campaigns. However, as time progressed, it happened that Gbonka, a subordinate general, challenged Sango's authority – giving him an ultimatum to vacate the throne. Angered by the general, Sango sought his sacred stones and ax from Oya, only to discover that it was defiled with the blood of her menses. This was a bad time, and it only made Gbonka more daring as Sango didn't dole out instant judgment as he normally would. In a bid to put down the erring subordinate, Sango raised his ax to summon lightning, but the ax had been stripped of its power due to the "unclean" blood from Oya's menses.

When he realized that Oya was responsible for his shame – it was a taboo for warriors to leave a challenge unattended as that marked an acceptance of defeat, Sango left the palace in a fury to the place where he could restore the power of his ax and stones.

His place of invocation, as it turned out, was a high rock facing the palace, and once he tried to restore the ax, he inevitably summoned lightning which struck the palace. Although some say it was a mistake, others say Sango intentionally struck the palace in anger as punishment to the people in the palace for watching while Gbonka's dare shamed him. Many died as the palace was ravaged by fire. Sango's two wives Oba and Osun, who lost their possessions in the fire, left the palace and returned to their homeland in anger and fear of Sango. In contrast, Oya, who realized her error and heard of Sango's demise, returned to her homeland in Nupe, where she drowned herself in the River Niger – also known as Odo Oya (River Oya).

Paths of Oya

139. Ọya Iyansan

This is about the Niger River known in Yoruba as Odo-Oya and its nine tributaries. As a Storm Goddess, Oya is seen as the queen and source of the Niger River.

140. Oya Bomi

This path of Oya is known as a Storm Goddess and can manifest winds from a gentle breeze up to hurricane force level winds and tornadoes.

141. Oya Afefere

This path of Oya is the Goddess of Change, as seen in both nature and life. Oya's changes are known to bring about are not slow and gradual; they are fierce, quick, and often appearing destructive.

142. Oya Igbale

This path of Oya is known for securing the gates to cemeteries. Most notably, she protects graves marked with a cross.

143. Oya Obinidodo

This is the path of Oya that maintains contact with the ancestors.

144. Oya Ira

This path of Oya was said to have entered the lower realm of Ira in search of Sango when she heard about his death.

145. Oya Funke

This path of Oya guards and protects the unborn or stillborn children's spirit, taking them under her wing as she guides them to the afterlife.

146. Oya Iya Efon

This path of Oya can be invoked when an illness has become terminal.

147. Oya Dira

This path of Oya can be found in marketplaces where businesses are conducted. She is noted for being a very shrewd businesswoman and is also good with horses.

148. Oya De

This path of Oya was an unbeatable warrior whose skills were unmatched. After her death, she became deified as an Orisha.

149. Oya Nike

This path of Oya is known as the champion of women, as she often meted judgment on their behalf. Women often ask Oya to give them the ability to choose their words so they can speak persuasively and powerfully.

150. Oya Obinidodo

Oya's machetes represent the sword of truth, cutting quickly to the truth of the matter and dealing out matters of equality and custom. As an agent of change, Oya will cut through all injustices, deceits, and dishonesty in her path. She will speak only truths, even when they are hard to hear.

151. Oya Dumi

This path of Oya is known to be a strong and fierce protector of women. She also protects children and spouses.

Oriki Oya

Oya yeba, Iya mesan, Iya Oyo.

Orun afefe iku lele bioke,

Ayaba gbogbo le'ya obinrin.

Ogo mi ano gbogbo gbun,

Orisa mi abaya

Oya ewa, Iya mesan.

Ase.

Translation:

Spirit of the wind, Mother of nine, Mother of Oyo,

The winds of heaven bring down the ancestors,

You're the queen of all women.

Always protect me with your strong medicine,

My guardian Spirit is the queen.

Spirit of the Wind and Mother of Nine.

So, let it be.

General Notes on Oya

- Oya is generally known as Iya Mesan. In Candomble, she is called Oia.

- Orisha Oya is known for her passion shown by ravaging storms and winds.

- Oya is an Orisha who hides the secrets of the dead so that they can dwell in peace.

- For sacrifice, Oya accepts unseasoned akara'je, which is mashed beans fried in palm oil.

Chapter 8: Dark Orishas III: The Healers

Generally, the dark Orishas are known for judgment, often executed fiercely. This is unlike the white Orishas associated with calm and counsel – it is ideally a lot easier to listen when you don't have to worry about being struck down for a slight. As it has been stated earlier, there are certain Orishas who lie in-between the white and dark Orishas. In the same vein, a white Orisha can at other times act as rashly as a dark Orisha but will always revert to being calm and easy to entreat. Among these special categories of Orishas that lie in-between are the healers. Every Orisha has a specific sphere of influence aside from generally being able to express power. The healers are Orishas that specialize in healing, albeit possessing the power to influence other aspects of life.

Among the Orishas who are known for healing is Osanyin the Orisha, who knows all about plants and herbal medicine, Nana Buluku, who is the patroness of women – her healing virtues are mostly channeled toward women and Babaluwaye, who is the Orisha of all diseases. While Osanyin and Nana Buluku are of the white Orishas, Babaluwaye is of the dark Orishas and is prone to a temper. Some say that Babaluwaye being the Orisha of all diseases, doesn't just take away illness or heal sick people. He also inflicts terrible sicknesses, especially on people who err. His cult was noted for engaging in terrifying warfare where they inflicted sicknesses at will, both as a means of punishment and for selfish reasons.

Babaluwaye

Babaluwaye is one of the most feared Orishas in the Yoruba culture. He goes by many names, such as Babalu Aye, Obaluwaiye, and is said to be the son of Nana Buluku. At other times, he is depicted as the male path of Nana Buluku. Babaluwaye is the Orisha of life and death and is the patron Orisha of sicknesses. Babaluwaye operates in two major ways: he either cures the sick or doles out judgment by inflicting sickness. Despite medicines (modern or local) being available, should Babaluwaye strike a person, there is a greater probability of death – except when he is appeased.

According to Yoruba traditions, Babaluwaye is depicted as a man covered in sores, representing his control over leprosy and smallpox. Although muscular, Babaluwaye walks with crutches and is covered from head to toe in raffia curtains, used to hide the sores covering his body. He is often seen with two dogs who ease the pain of his sores by licking them constantly.

Based on his depiction, Babaluwaye is syncretized in Santeria with the Catholic Saint Lazarus, a known leper who was constantly seen with two dogs that licked his sores. In Santeria, Babaluwaye's day of celebration is held on the 17th of December in tandem with Saint Lazarus. In the same vein, he is associated with the number 17 and is mostly worshipped on Thursdays.

As the Orisha of diseases, Babaluwaye resides in a clay pot decked with cowrie shells. This pot is kept in a dark, calm place where he is not to be disturbed. Only his priest may invoke him using 18 cowrie shells placed on the clay pot. Should anyone try to summon Babaluwaye without being a priest, such a person risks becoming inflicted with terrible diseases leading to death.

According to Yoruba stories concerning Babaluwaye, he was initially a handsome prince revered by many. However, he was unruly – rather than respecting elder Orishas, he preferred to act on his own. Because of this, his attitude drew upon him different impurities scattered across the Yoruba realm. These impurities turned into sicknesses and diseases, which he eventually began traveling about with.

As he had been disfigured by impurities and was losing respect – even among his sons, Babaluwaye sought help from other Orishas, but none responded to him due to his track record of disrespect. Fortunately for him, Eshu, the Orishas messenger, took pity on him and brought him before Orunmila. Orunmila was not pleased with Babaluwaye's case and voiced his opinion to Eshu, saying, "You always bring me the hard ones, but I will speak to Ifa concerning him."

According to Ifa, Babaluwaye had been rejected due to his unruly and disobedient nature. However, Ifa told him he would be accepted and even celebrated in a strange land – he had already been exiled from home due to the impurities that stuck to him like scars. However, to get to the strange land, he would need to offer a sacrifice of grains (different types) and travel with a dog which was to be his companion at all times.

Babaluwaye, who had grown remorseful, appreciated Orunmila and acted as he was instructed. Helped by Eshu, he got the dog he needed and made his journey down to Dahomey. When he got there, he encountered a people with an unruly king that deemed himself a god and acted as he pleased. However, at the sight of Babaluwaye, the king fell to the ground and begged for forgiveness. It was as though he saw in Babaluwaye what would befall him if he continued in his unruly ways. He was prayed for by Babaluwaye, and he turned a new leaf to the relief of his people. Babaluwaye was greatly celebrated for his influence over the king and was seen as an emblem of consequences. When a person acts without caution or reason, there are bound to be consequences. Babaluwaye, who started as unruly, learned the hard way, but helped by Orunmila and Eshu, he overcame the consequences. He grew to become a gentle person with only his inner beauty and good character left. He was greatly disfigured on the outside due to the impurities he'd drawn toward himself. As the story goes, Babaluwaye ultimately became a king in Dahomey and ruled with wisdom.

Babaluwaye's Children

All devotees of Babaluwaye are known as his children. Each child of Babaluwaye specializes in healing - both spiritual and medical healing. Usually, they, just like Babaluwaye, have suffered one or more forms of skin disease in their younger years. As children of Babaluwaye, they possess both the ability to heal and the power to inflict terrible sickness on anyone who incurs their wrath. Usually, Babaluwaye's children are jovial but can easily switch to anger. Babaluwaye possesses fearsome powers, but that doesn't stop him from being calm - just as his children are joyful.

Invoking Babaluwaye

Babaluwaye, although a dark Orisha, is the one to call upon when faced with sicknesses - especially the terminal ones. As a healer, Babaluwaye knows whether to heal the sick or to allow a terminally sick person to pass on without pain. As with medical doctors who know when to recommend euthanasia - medically induced death due to terminal illnesses, Babaluwaye can help a sick person die in peace. This only happens when Babaluwaye himself has deemed the person's case as irredeemable - where death is inevitable. Where there is hope for survival, Babaluwaye would offer to heal as expected. A proof of his power to heal has been shown in the Yoruba legend where Sango was sick and could not be healed by any other. He visited Babaluwaye to heal him of his sickness, and he was promptly back to full health.

When invoking Babaluwaye, it is important to offer either roasted corn, black beans, dry grains, tobacco, or wine. He also welcomes meat sacrifices of vultures or other carcass-feeding birds. Place your offering before him on an altar decked with sacred stones and a statue of him. Yellow or purple candles are to be lit around the altar before you begin your prayer - strictly for mercy. For certainty and avoidance of error, have an experienced devotee do this on your behalf. The reason for this is that apart from the prayers, there will be a need for divination using either Diloggun or the Obi system of divination, and Babaluwaye only permits his own to invoke him.

To begin praying, it is expected that you begin with a recital such as this:

> *Babaluwaye, the god of all sicknesses and those who are sick.*
>
> *I call upon you, have mercy on us.*
>
> *We are your children, have mercy on us,*
>
> *Keep sicknesses far away from our homes, and protect us - your children - from all plague.*
>
> *Thank you, father, for you have answered, and you will heal us.*

Paths of Babaluwaye

Babaluwaye has an average of 60 paths, with Sopona being one of his most fearsome paths. Sopona, which is the path that establishes him as the Orisha of smallpox, is rarely spoken of. This is done out of fear of being inflicted by smallpox, which was fatal in olden times, and out of reverence for Babaluwaye, with other paths more dignifying. He is best known as Babaluwaye, the father or king of the world, as this is more respectful and gives him a wider range of influence. However, here are a few paths of Babaluwaye:

152. Babaluwaye Asojano

This path of Babaluwaye speaks from Odu Ojuani, and he helps with warnings about impending famine, droughts, and epidemics. Some say that Asojano was disfigured when elders made use of unclean knives for his scarification ritual. Because of their error, Babaluwaye Asojano brought pestilence to the world. Asojano is the patron Orisha of persons treated unjustly.

153. Babaluwaye Asoyin Arara

This path of Babaluwaye is known as the father of the rain, which can kill due to its extremely hot temperature. This is the path that was said to have killed many with smallpox.

154. Babaluwaye Alua

This path of Babaluwaye is known for his wisdom

155. Babaluwaye Baba Arugbo

This is an aged path that appears as an elderly man – he is known as the ancient father.

156. Babaluwaye Afimaye

This path of Babaluwaye is known as the gravedigger and walks hand in hand with Orisha Oya, who rules over the dead.

157. Babaluwaye N'yone Nanu

This is a female path of Babaluwaye Asojano. She is always draped in black and dwells in ceiba trees.

158. Babaluwaye Molu

This is a path of Babaluwaye associated with hunting. He always makes use of a bow and arrow lined in leopard skin.

159. Babaluwaye Aberu Shaban

This is a male path of Babaluwaye, who eats intestines. He delivers food to the children of Babaluwaye Asojano

160. Babaluwaye Abokun

This is a male path of Babaluwaye and is identified as a farmer. He is known for fertilizing the earth and always walks with three companions, a lion, a crocodile, and the maja.

161. Babaluwaye Adu Kake

This is a path of Babaluwaye in Cuba and takes the form of a dog and lives naked in the mountains. He is said to possess a man's body with the head of a dog.

162. Babaluwaye Adan Wan

This is a male path of Babaluwaye, who kills anyone who offends him.

163. Babaluwaye Afrosan

This is a male path of Babaluwaye that uses the air for his activities.

164. Babaluwaye Afisinu Sanaje

This is a male path of Babaluwaye, who lives in the marketplace. He appears as a mouse and rarely speaks.

165. Babaluwaye Ajidenudo

This is another male path of Babaluwaye, who takes the form of a midget. He dwells with Osanyin and encourages witchcraft.

166. Babaluwaye Amabo

This is a male path of Babaluwaye, who inflicts offenders with chickenpox and elephantiasis.

167. Babaluwaye Apadado

This is a warrior path of Babaluwaye, who lives in anthills.

168. Babaluwaye Bayanana

This is a female path of Babaluwaye and is the patroness Orisha of virgin daughters of Babaluwaye Asojano.

169. Babaluwaye Ason'tuno

This is a male path of Babaluwaye and is known for traveling around with all diseases accompanying him.

Differences between Osanyin and Babaluwaye

At times, Osanyin is often misconceived as Babaluwaye due to the similarity of their office. However, both Orishas are different and operate in different ways. Among such differences are:

- Osanyin is strictly the Orisha of plants and herbal medicine, while Babaluwaye is the Orisha of sicknesses and diseases he can inflict or heal.

- Osanyin operates majorly via his staff of power, while Babaluwaye operates via his raffia curtains which he uses as a broom to sweep away sicknesses and disease.

- Osanyin heals without discrimination, but Babaluwaye's cult has been noted for inflicting sicknesses for selfish purposes. As such, they do not heal everyone – especially those upon whom they inflict sicknesses.

- Babaluwaye helps the terminally sick to pass on in peace, while Osanyin only applies plant medicine to help alleviate the pain of the sick.

- Babaluwaye is a dark Orisha possessing traits peculiar to white Orishas – he and his children are jovial. Osanyin, on the other hand, is a white Orisha.

Chapter 9: Talking to the Orishas With Diloggun

Communicating with the Orisha is possible. Orunmila ensured this when he taught mankind divination using the Ifa divination system. He gave select persons the means to commune with the Orishas, invoking their presence and powers over situations. But then, divination did not start with Orunmila and indeed started with Olodumare.

According to Yoruba legend, Olodumare summoned his children to a summit. Once they appeared before him and greeted him duly, Olodumare began speaking:

"My children, listen to me, for I am here to let you know things that must be. Know that my laws are yours to obey, and every task I give to you must be accomplished. I have borne you all for a purpose, which is to continue the work of creation I have started. I have finished my part, and all that is left is for you all to continue in my stead. You will continue to influence the growth of this planet I have created, and you will pave the way for those coming - the future generations.

Know that I will no longer take part in the growth of this planet, neither will I influence those on the planet. You will do all that for me. Your assignment will be to teach every living thing my will, my ways, and how they can reach out to me. First, they will come to you and report their case to you. Then, you will bring their requests to me so that I may tell you what to do for them. This is not a hard thing, but I must warn you - never try to carry out another person's assignment. You all have your assignments. Do them diligently, and don't try to carry out the assignment of any other.

Today, I give you the way to speak to me and teach those on the planet how to speak to me. Today, I give you Diloggun (16 cowrie shells) - use them as an oracle to speak to the people on the planet. Diloggun shall be your mouth to speak to all, telling them of my will in all cases."

Once Olodumare had spoken, he established how the Orishas could communicate with him first, then communicate within themselves, and last, how they should communicate with mankind. With Diloggun as a divination system, the power to recall the hidden past and tell the future's secrets was born in the Yoruba culture.

Types of Divination Systems

In Santeria, the divination system established by Olodumare is known as Diloggun. However, the Yoruba culture identifies this divination system as Odu Orisha Erindilogun, which signifies that it is a divination system of 16 cowrie shells. However, there are different forms of divination. Taking from the words of Olodumare when he said, "your assignment will be to teach every living thing my will, my ways and how they can reach out to me," notice this was a hint at each Orisha being able to divine. Osun has her means of divination, just like Orunmila has his means of divination - the widely recognized Ifa divination system. One thing, however, is common among the forms of divination, and that is that most utilize cowrie shells. Olodumare established divination using 16 cowrie shells, and how each Orisha utilizes these 16 cowrie shells determines the form of such divination.

Among the forms of divination known to the Yoruba religion are:

170. Diloggun

Diloggun is also known as Odu Orisha Erindilogun. Here, the 16 cowrie shells used for divination are only accessible to initiated priests (Santeros) and priestesses (Santeras) in the Yoruba Santerian religion. Only those who have been initiated and have gone through adequate training can read the 16 cowrie shells. With Diloggun, 256 signs can be read in the cowrie shells. Each sign comes with a unique parable or story attached to it. These parables are used to give counsel and determine the course of a person's life. The past, present, and future are laid bare during readings, and once counsel is given, it is left to the individual to act upon such counsel. The Diloggun is very similar to the Ifa divination system.

171. Odu Ifa

Odu Ifa refers to a collection of prayers and stories passed down by Orunmila to his priests and priestesses, who likewise pass down the knowledge from generation to generation. In Odu Ifa, 16 major books are subdivided into 16 minor books of secrets. There are 256 Odu in this divination system, and they hold the solution to all possible circumstances. With Odu Ifa, there is a divining accuracy of at least 90%, and with it, counsel and wisdom can be given concerning any circumstance brought before Ifa.

172. Obi

This divination system makes use of five pieces of kola nuts. The pieces are thrown onto a divining cloth, and a divining priest or priestess reads the signs they display. To a considerable extent, it is deemed as one of the easiest forms of divination among the three.

General Notes on Divination

Divination is a sacred tradition in the Yoruba culture that helps to determine a person's fate. This isn't based on just foretelling of the future but also calling into account the past's deeds via divine hindsight. Once the past and present have been laid bare, the future can then be foretold accurately.

Consequent to the fact that divination is a sacred art, only experienced devotees, priests, and priestesses of the Orishas are permitted to engage in it. Santeria does not allow a non-initiate to practice Diloggun. The knowledge of divining in Santeria is closely guarded so that only generic information is offered to inquisitive minds - but secrets are only known by initiates being trained to practice Diloggun. In the same vein, the Obi system of divination and Odu Ifa strictly warn that only an experienced devotee is to engage in divination. The reason is not farfetched - there are many possibilities (256), and not all those possibilities are good. Negative possibilities can occur, and it takes an experienced mind to be clear of such possibilities. Also, there is a greater chance of misreading the signs seen in divination when done by an amateur, let alone a non-initiate. Hence, to avoid errors and possible terror, it is advised that a person gets initiated and is duly taught before engaging in any divination systems. Likewise, you can seek the assistance of a practicing diviner rather than risk error and its attendant consequences.

Tools for Divination

Diloggun being a divination system of cowrie shells, require certain things to be in place before any divination can be done. By default, it is expected that an Oba - the general name given to divining priests and priestesses of Santeria, possess a bag of cowrie shells to be used for divination. Sixteen cowrie shells are used for divination, but the Oba must possess up to 21 cowrie shells. When divining for

Eshu the Orishas messenger, 21 cowrie shells are expected to be in his possession. In comparison, 18 cowrie shells are expected to be in his possession when divining for other Orishas.

173. Divining Bone

Aside from the cowrie shells used in divination, a small bone is required to help read the shells' signs. This bone symbolizes the dividing line between good and bad, and because of this, it is essential to every divination attempt.

174. Divining Platform

Diloggun is a divination system that specializes in throwing down cowrie shells and then reading the signs made by them. However, the shells are not to be thrown in any manner. Neither are they to be thrown just anywhere. It is expected that the cowrie shells or kola nuts are thrown onto a divining platform for all forms of divination. This could either be a cloth - which is mostly white, a table, wooden tray, or a raffia mat.

175. Divining Cloth

For every divination system, there is sacred clothing worn before any attempt at divination. Like the divining cloth used as a platform, an Oba is adorned in white clothing - while in other contexts, the cloth worn is red. The divining cloth worn is often decked with cowrie shells and is blessed as a form of consecration to the Orishas before it is used/worn. Diviners are expected to be shed of any items such as a ring or other jewelry, as these would impair the accuracy of their divination.

176. Efun

This is a ball made of powdered eggshells held in the palm. It represents Ire (blessing) in divination.

177. Ota

This is a black rocky item that fits into the palm. It represents Ofo (misfortune) in divination.

178. Cleansing

Generally, the tools used for divination are cleansed and consecrated via prayers and a blood sacrifice. This ensures that all impurities are washed out of the items, leaving them clean to be used by the Orishas for responding to mankind.

179. Timing of Divination

Divining only happens from dawn until the early hours of dusk. It is believed that Osun, who is a principal Orisha of divination, leaves divining once it is dusk and only returns to it once the day breaks. Hence, for accuracy, it is advised to divine before dusk.

Intention in Divination

Recalling a lesson from Orisha Ogun, who turned his back on the people he swore to protect due to their carelessness in invoking him, it stands to reason that the Orishas respond only to sincerity. Trying to invoke the Orishas for fun is a risky gamble and, at the same time, a futile endeavor as they would usually not respond. No matter how serious a case, the Orishas will not respond where it is perceived there is an iota of insincerity or lack of seriousness. Where intent is in doubt, the Orishas have no business responding.

The intention is important both to the diviner and the person requesting divination. The diviner must, first of all, be pure and likewise ready to divine - receive the counsel of the Orishas for such divination to be accurate. Where a diviner is impure or not ready, the cowrie shells will fall into indiscernible patterns until the diviner has done the needful preparation. In this case, preparation isn't just outwardly displayed but is also a matter of the heart or sincere intent.

In the same vein, a person requesting divination must prove to be sincere and willing to carry out the Orishas' instructions and must not lie to the diviner - lying is tantamount to insincerity. Where a client is insincere or has no plan of abiding by the Orishas' counsel, such a client will get no response from the Orishas. Thus, it would be a waste of effort and time to the diviner and the client. Due to the uncertainty surrounding people's intent, priests are asked if clients are willing to obey the Orishas before they progress further into divining with the cowrie shells.

Chapter 10: Understanding What the Shell Mouths Say

Every Yoruba inclined religion engages in divination - it is foundational to the entire religion and serves as the basis for moral principles. Yoruba people, in general, depend greatly on what the Orishas say before making decisions. Among the devotees, certain people are selected to undergo sacred training for a while before they're permitted to invoke the Orishas via divination.

Although a great deal of knowledge about divination is kept sacred within the confines of cults dedicated to the Orishas, there is still sufficient knowledge available to the public. All knowledge about divination was initially sacred, and no person outside the cult could learn or know the ways of divination. However, as the years progressed into recent times, some elders - devotees with great experience in divining deemed it fit to make certain knowledge known about divination. This was done to preserve the knowledge of divination and garner interest in the Orisha tradition. Westernization brought about a wind of extinction that threatened to erase the Yoruba people's history, culture, and religion. First, it began with slavery and oppressive regimes, but over time a new strategy has played out, and it is none other than distracting the newer generations with the thrills of foreign cultures.

The aim of preserving Yoruba tradition was largely achieved. But it didn't end there. Aside from preserving the ancient traditions, this sacred knowledge gave power to interested people so that they could rightly divine and determine the course of their personal lives without having to call on a priest. Of course, it is advised that a priest is consulted for divination of greater accuracy, but it doesn't hurt to be able to foretell one's own destiny - even if it's just surface information.

What the Shell Mouths Say

Cowrie shells have always been of great value in the Yoruba culture since their inception. Aside from being used as money in the olden times, it remained a vital tool of divination. To some, the cowrie shells serve as the third eye to gain access into the realm of divinities and our ancestors. This is a timeless realm filled with endless knowledge and wisdom that can help us live with greater fulfillment. With the cowrie shells, we gain access into all ages; the past, present, and future.

According to Yoruba tradition, the cowrie shells serve as the Orishas' voice, and they speak uniquely. To make them speak, the cowrie shells are gently tossed onto a divining platform. Depending on how they fall and the pattern they create, the diviner then reads their interpretation based on sacred knowledge about the cowrie shells' patterns.

Recalling the types of divination, the interpretation is given to the patterns made by the cowrie shells differ. For instance, the Obi system of divination interprets the fallen patterns as either "yes" or "no," while the Diloggun system of divination gives more than just "yes" or "no" interpretations.

Obi Divination

In the Obi system of divination, kola nuts are used in place of cowrie shells, and questions are thrown to the oracle in ways that would generate a "yes" or "no" response. For instance, a person could ask, "Will I prosper if I do this?" rather than "What should I do?" This way, the oracle recognizes the free will and intent of a divining client. Where questions are put straightforwardly, it becomes easy for the oracle to respond appropriately.

In the Obi system of divination, four pieces of kola nuts are traditionally used, and their fallen patterns are placed into five categories. However, diviners of the Obi system in the United States utilize cowrie shells in place of kola nuts, but the interpretation strategy is the same.

The four shells or kola nuts represent the secrets of the past and the future. Here, the diviner places the shells in his/her hand and prays over the question you've posed. Free praying, the diviner then blows into the shells and tosses them onto the divining cloth or table and interprets the pattern shown. Where there is uncertainty about an interpretation, the whole exercise is repeated.

The five categories of interpretation are defined as follows:

1. Alaafia

Four shell mouths facing up; as the name implies, it is the response of peace and certainty. It is the oracle saying "yes" to your question. When this happens, your heart's desires may be granted a lot faster than expected. While this is a solid guarantee, you're expected to make one more toss of the shells to confirm the first response. You're expected to see a second alaafia as proof.

2. Etawa

Three shell mouths face up, while one shell mouth faces down; this is an undecided response. It is a "maybe" due to the existence of one shell contradicting three others. Etawa could also be considered as a "yes," albeit shaky. Hence, it is expected to make another throw to get a more decisive answer.

3. Ejife

Two shell mouths face down, while two shell mouths face down; this is also a solid "yes" due to the balance between the shells. Here, there is no need for a confirmatory throw.

4. Okanran

One shell mouth faces up, while three shell mouths face down; this is a firm "no" as three shells contradict one. This indicates that there is a great deal of work to do before success is achieved.

5. Oyekun

Four shell mouths face down; this represents total darkness. It is the strongest "no" and requires a ritual cleansing to churn out the negative energies surrounding the matter you tabled before the oracle.

Diloggun Divination

The cowrie shells in Diloggun are consecrated through blood sacrifice and possess deeper meanings than the kola nuts used in the Obi system of divination. Diloggun, a variant of Odu Erindilogun, is practiced in Santeria and requires initiation before anyone can learn the rudiments of divining with the shells.

To get started divining, a diviner is expected to give praises to Olodumare, Egun, and the ancestors first. Once this is done, Elegba, the messenger path of Eshu, is to be invoked alongside the Orisha that is to be consulted, e.g., Osun. An offering must be in place before going further to appease Elegba and the Orisha you're consulting. Note that the offering must be specific to the consulted Orisha - don't give an offering meant for Yemoja to Ogun; it's a grievous error. It is expected that you give a part of every offering to Elegba so he can keep the channel between you and your Orisha open.

Once a diviner is done the needful in giving praises and offerings, attention must be paid to the pattern in which the cowrie shells fall. In Diloggun, the patterns of the shell are classed into two-parent Odu and composite Odu. The parent Odu appears after the first toss of the shells, while the composite Odu appears after the second toss. Both Odu makes up the overall pattern of the shells and is to be interpreted as one. For instance, where the first toss produces five as the parent Odu, and the second toss produces nine as the composite Odu, the pattern made is 5-9. This is then to be interpreted either as a blessing or misfortune.

To get the interpretation, the tools known as Efun and Ota are used. Both items are placed in the divining client's hands, who then shakes his hands and divides both items into separate hands. Both hands are to be firmly closed until the diviner asks the client to unveil the left or right hand.

Once the diviner has read the pattern, the numbers will determine which hand is to be opened. If the Efun is revealed, the interpretation veers toward blessings, but the interpretation is nothing but misfortune if the Ota is unveiled. However, divining doesn't end there. Inquiries have to be made to determine the source of either the blessings or the misfortunes. Here, the diviner would have to converse with the client and interpret to arrive at a conclusion. Once the source of either blessing or misfortune is revealed, the diviner would then make further inquiries to determine what sacrifice or offering is to be made either in thanksgiving or plea for mercy.

Each Odu is represented by the number of shells that face up after falling onto the divining platform. Hence, where ten shells fall face up, the Odu is equal to ten. There are 16 basic patterns or parent Odu that could be read from each throw of the cowrie shells. However, underneath these 16 patterns are 256 composite Odu that could be read. The 16 basic patterns include:

- **Okanran** – A single shell mouth faces up; it means hurt no one

- **Eji Oko** – Two shell mouths face up; it means feel no hate nor seek destruction for others

- **Eta Ogunda** – Three shell mouths face up, it means seek no vengeance

- **Irosun** – Four shell mouths face up, it means do not slander nor trap anyone

- **Ose** – Five shell mouths face up, it means avoid envy toward anyone and anything

- **Obara** – Six shell mouths face up, it means do not lie

- **Odi** – Seven shell mouths face up, it means do not be corrupt neither should you corrupt anyone

- **Eji Onile** – Eight shell mouths face up; it means to respect the secrets of others and use your head wisely

- **Osa** – Nine shell mouths face up; it means to avoid being fake with others

- **Ofun** – Ten shell mouths face up, it means do not steal, curse or swear falsely

- **Owanrin** – Eleven shell mouths face up, it means do not kill or ruin other people's lives and be grateful for good done to you

- **Ejila Sebora** – Twelve shell mouths face up; it means avoid tragedies and scandals

- **Eji Ologbon** – Thirteen shell mouths face up, this is also known as metala, and it means to respect the ancestors

- **Ika** – Fourteen shell mouths face up, it is also known as merinla, and it means do not spread corruption, evil, or disease

- **Ogbegunda** – Fifteen shell mouths face up, also known as marunla and means respect the elders, children, father, and mother

- **Alaafia** – Sixteen shell mouths face up, it is known as merindilogun, and it means that if you listen to this counsel, you will find peace and boldness when standing before Olodumare.

- **Opira** – This is the seventeenth pattern where no mouth faces up, and it means the reading is inaccurate. This could be the fault of either the diviner or the client.

Conclusion

Diloggun as a means of divination provides insight into a person's life and can help redefine destiny. It is a means of communication with the Orishas who have existed before creation and will remain even after this world's end. The Yoruba people believe in a proverb that says, *"What an elder sees whilst seated, a young man cannot see even if he stands at the peak of the highest mountain."* The Orishas have existed before time. It is only wise that they're sought for their counsel and power – after all, they are the ancient ones whose wisdom and powers transcend our space and time.

Here's another book by Mari Silva that you might like

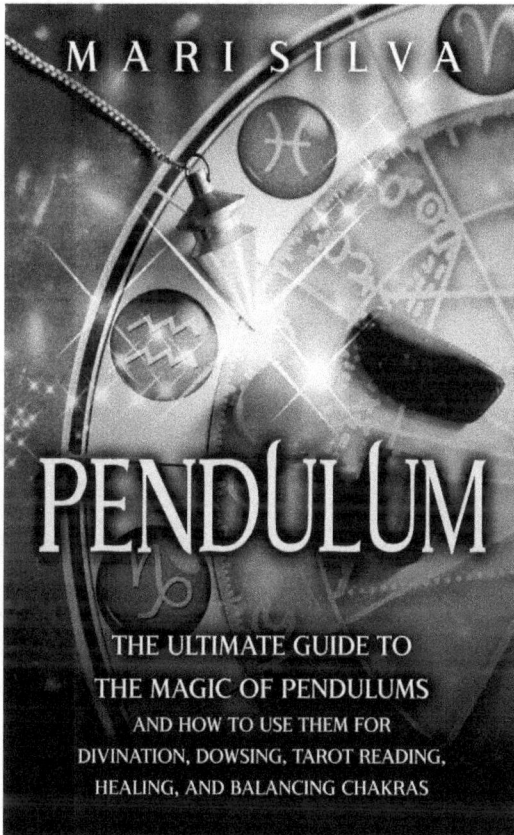

MARI SILVA

PENDULUM

THE ULTIMATE GUIDE TO
THE MAGIC OF PENDULUMS
AND HOW TO USE THEM FOR
DIVINATION, DOWSING, TAROT READING,
HEALING, AND BALANCING CHAKRAS

Your Free Gift (only available for a limited time)

Thanks for getting this book! If you want to learn more about various spirituality topics, then join Mari Silva's community and get a free guided meditation MP3 for awakening your third eye. This guided meditation mp3 is designed to open and strengthen ones third eye so you can experience a higher state of consciousness. Simply visit the link below the image to get started.

https://spiritualityspot.com/meditation

References

Falola, Toyin (2016) | Encyclopedia of the Yoruba

J. Omosade Awolalu | Yoruba Beliefs & Sacrificial Rites

Adeoye C.L. (1989) | Igbagbo ati Esin Yoruba

William Bascom | Sixteen Cowries

Idowu E.B. (1962) | Olodumare; God in Yoruba Belief

Harold Courlander | Tales of Yoruba Gods & Heroes

Lynch, Patricia Ann (2018) | African Mythology, A to Z

William Bascom (1991) | Ifa Divination: Communication Between Gods and Men in West Africa

Ifaloju A. | Iwori Meji; Ifa Speaks on Righteousness

James J. Kulevich | The Odu of Lucumi; Information on all 256 Odu Ifa

Fagbemijo Amosun Fakayode (2012) | Ori Mi Gbe Mi; Ori Support Me

Makinde M.A. (1985) | A Philosophical Analysis of the Yoruba Concepts of Ori and Human Destiny

Ifaloju A. (2007) | Ori – The Divine Container of Destiny, Character & Potential, Seed of the Creator

Elebuibon, Yemi; Adventures of Obatala

James T. Houk (1995) | Spirits, Blood, and Drums; the Orisha Religion of Trinidad

John Mason | Orin Orisa; Songs for Selected Heads

Robert Marcel (1997) | Ogun Worship in Idanre; Iron and Identity in a Yoruba Town

Adeoye C.L. (1989) |Igbagbo ati Esin Yoruba

Robert D. Pelton (1989) | The Trickster in West Africa; A Study of Mythic Irony and Sacred Delight

Alamoja Yoruba (2019) | Esu is Not Satan; Who Esu Is and Who He Is Not

Murrell, Nathaniel S. (2009) | Afro-Caribbean Religions; An Introduction to Their Historical, Cultural and Sacred Traditions.

Monaghan (2014) | Encyclopedia of Goddesses and Heroines

Akalatunde, Osunyemi (2005) | Ona Agbani; The Ancient Path – Understanding and Implementing the Ways of Our Ancestors

Chief Yagbe Awolowo Only (2016) | Deities and Divination

 The Yoruba Religious Concepts; Understanding the Belief Concepts of the Lucumi Faith

"African Poems – Oral Poetry from Africa." Africanpoems.net

"HERITAGE: Be Mindful of Your Self-Talk = It's a Conversation with the Universe..." Chief Yagbe Awolowo Onilu, yagbeonilu.com.

"Ọmọ Oòduà." Ọmọ Oòduà, ooduarere.com.

"OWULAKODA Blog." OWULAKODA Blog, owulakoda.wordpress.com.

Menoukha Case. (2008). Santería: A Practical Guide to Afro-Caribbean Magic, and: Santería Stories (review). Callaloo, 32(1), 307–313. https://muse.jhu.edu/article/260434

Orisha Worshippers. (n.d.). https://www.bop.gov/foia/docs/orishamanual.pdf

"Santería," The Lucumí Way. (n.d.). Retrieved from https://hwpi.harvard.edu/files/pluralism/files/santeria-the_lucumi_way_0.pdf

Yoruba | people. (2019). In Encyclopædia Britannica. https://www.britannica.com/topic/Yoruba

www.ingramcontent.com/pod-product-compliance
Lightning Source LLC
Chambersburg PA
CBHW071856090426
42811CB00004B/630